Y0-CBI-486

THE POWER OF GOD

Nobody has
ever heard of opening
the eyes of a man born blind.
If this man were not from God,
he could do nothing.
(John 9:32-33)

THE POWER OF GOD

Reverend Dr. Jaerock Lee

The Power of God

ISBN: 89-7557-075-4

Urim Books
851, Guro-dong, Guro-gu
Seoul, Republic of Korea

Edited by Geumsun Vin
Published in Seoul, Korea, by Seongkeon Vin
Manufactured in Republic of Korea
First Edition October 2005

Note on the Text :

All scripture quotations are taken from the New International Version(NIV) of the Holy Bible unless otherwise stated.

PREFACE

Praying that by the power of God the Creator and the gospel of Jesus Christ, may all people experience the fiery work of the Holy Spirit...

I give all thanks to Father God, who has blessed us to publish into a single work the messages from the 11th Two-week Special Revival Meeting conducted in May 2003 – held under the theme "Power" – at which a number of testimonies greatly glorified God.

Since 1993, soon after the tenth anniversary of the founding, God began nurturing the members of Manmin Joong-ang Church to possess true faith and become spiritual people through the annual Two-week Special Revival Meetings.

At the 1999 Revival Meeting He allowed trials of blessings so that Manmin members would come to realize the significance of the true gospel, accomplish the law in love, and resemble our Lord who manifested wondrous power. At the dawn of a new millennium in 2000, in order for all people around the world to experience the power of God the Creator, the gospel of Jesus Christ, and the fiery work of the Holy Spirit, God blessed us to broadcast the

Revival Meetings live via the Moogoonghwa satellite and the Internet. In 2003, audiences from approximately 300 churches within Korea and fifteen countries participated in the Revival Meeting.

The Power of God has attempted to introduce the process in which one meets God and receives His power, the different levels of power, the Most High Power of Creation that goes beyond the limit permissible for a creature human being, and the places at which His power is manifested.

The power of God the Creator descends upon an individual as much as he resembles God who is the light. Furthermore, when he becomes one in spirit with God, he can manifest the kind of power Jesus manifested. This is because in John 15:7, our Lord tells us, *"If you remain in me and my words remain in you, ask whatever you wish, and it will be given to you."*

For I have personally experienced the joy and happiness in the freedom from seven years' diseases and agony, in order to be a servant of power who resembles the Lord, I fasted and prayed a number of days and times after I was called to be a servant of the Lord. Jesus tells us in Mark 9:23, *"'If you can?' Everything is possible for him who believes."* I also believed and prayed because I held fast to Jesus' promise, *"[Anyone] who has faith in me will do what I have been doing. He will do greater things than these, because I am going to the Father"* (John 14:12). As a result, through the annual Revival Meetings, God has shown us astonishing signs and wonders and given us countless healings and answers. Furthermore, during the second week of the 2003 Revival Meeting, God focused the manifestation of His power on those who were blind, unable to walk, hear, and talk.

Even if medical science has advanced and continues to make progress, it is almost impossible for people who have lost sight or hearing to be healed. The almighty God, however, manifested His power so that when I prayed only from the pulpit, the work of the power of creation could renew dead nerves and cells, and people would come to see, hear, and speak. In addition, bent spines were straightened, and stiffened bones became loose so that people could throw away their crutches, canes, and wheelchairs, and get up, leap, and walk.

The miraculous work of God also transcends time and space. People who attended the Revival Meetings via satellite and on the Internet also experienced the power of God, and their testimonies are submitted even to this day.

This is why the messages from the 2003 Revival Meeting – at which countless people were reborn by the Word of the truth, received a new life, salvation, answers, and healing, experienced the power of God, and greatly glorified Him – have been published into a single work.

I give special thanks to Geumsun Vin, Director of Editorial Bureau, and her staff and Translation Bureau for their hard work and dedication.

May each of you experience the power of God the Creator, the gospel of Jesus Christ, and the fiery work of the Holy Spirit, and may joy and happiness overflow in your life – all this I pray in the name of our Lord!

Jaerock Lee

The Author

Rev. Dr. Jaerock Lee

He was born in Muan, Jeonnam Province, Republic of Korea, in 1943. In his twenties, Rev. Dr. Lee had suffered from a variety of incurable diseases for seven years and awaited death with no hope for recovery. One day in the spring of 1974, however, he was led to a church by his sister and when he knelt down to pray, the living God immediately healed him of all his diseases.

From the moment Rev. Dr. Lee met the Living God through that wonderful experience, he has loved God with all his heart and sincerity, and in 1978 was called to be a servant of God. He prayed fervently so that he could clearly understand the will of God and wholly accomplish it, and obeyed all the Word of God. In 1982, he founded Manmin Joong-ang Church in Seoul, S. Korea, and countless works of God, including miraculous healings and wonders, have been taking place at his church.

In 1986, Rev. Dr. Lee was ordained as a pastor at the Annual Assembly of Jesus' Sungkyul Church of Korea, and four years later in 1990, his sermons began to be broadcast on the Far East Broadcasting Company, the Asia Broadcast Station, and the Washington Christian Radio System to Australia, Russia, the Philippines, and many more.

Three years later in 1993, Manmin Joong-ang Church was selected as one of the "World's Top 50 Churches" by the *Christian World* magazine (US) and he received an Honorary Doctorate of Divinity from Christian Faith College, Florida, USA, and in 1996 a Ph. D. in Ministry from Kingsway Theological Seminary, Iowa, USA.

Since 1993, Rev. Dr. Lee has taken the lead in world mission through many overseas crusades in the USA, Tanzania, Argentina, Uganda, Japan, Pakistan, Kenya, the Philippines, Honduras, India, Russia, Germany and Peru, and in 2002 he was called a "Worldwide pastor" by major Christian newspapers in Korea for his work in various overseas Great United Crusades.

As of October 2005, Manmin Joong-ang Church is a congregation of more than 90,000 members and 3,600 domestic and overseas branch churches throughout the globe, and has so far commissioned more than 77 missionaries to 20 countries, including the United States, Russia, Germany, Canada, Japan, China, France, India, Kenya, and many more.

To this day, Rev. Dr. Lee has written 39 books, including bestsellers *Tasting Eternal Life before Death, The Message of the Cross, The Measure of Faith, Heaven I & II,* and *Hell,* and his works have been translated into more than 16 languages.

Rev. Dr. Lee is currently founder and president of a number of missionary organizations, including Manmin TV, Global Christian Network (GCN), The World Christian Doctors Network (WCDN), Manmin International Seminary, The Nation Evangelization Paper, The United Holiness Church of Korea, The Light & Salt Mission, and Manmin World Mission.

INTRODUCTION

A must-read that serves as an essential guide by which one can possess true faith and experience the wondrous power of God

I give all thanks and glory to God, who has led us to publish into a single work the messages from The 11th Two-week Special Revival Meeting with Rev. Dr. Jaerock Lee in May 2003, which took place in the midst of God's great and wondrous power.

The Power of God will engulf you in grace and poignancy, as it contains nine messages from the Revival Meeting that was held under the theme "Power," as well as testimonies from a number of individuals who directly experienced the power of the living God and the gospel of Jesus Christ.

In the First Message, "To Believe in God," the identity of God, what it is to believe in Him, and the ways in which we can meet and experience Him are described.

In the Second Message, "To Believe in the Lord," the purpose of Jesus' coming to the earth, why only Jesus is our Savior, and why we receive salvation and answers when we believe in the Lord Jesus, are discussed.

Message Three, "A Vessel More Beautiful than a Jewel," elaborates on what it takes to be a precious, noble, and beautiful vessel in God's sight, as well as the blessings that descend on such a vessel.

The Fourth Message, "The Light," explains the spiritual light, what we need to do in order to meet God who is the light, and the blessings we will receive when we walk in the light.

The Fifth Message, "The Power of the Light," delves into the four different levels of God's power that are manifested by creature human beings through a variety of colors of light, as well as the real-life testimonies of diverse sorts of healing manifested at each level. Furthermore, by introducing the Most High Power of Creation, the unlimited power of God and the ways in which we can receive the power of the light are explained in detail.

Based on the process in which the man born blind received sight upon meeting Jesus and the testimonies from a number of people who have received sight and been healed of bad eyesight, the Sixth Message, "The Eyes of the Blind Will Open," will help you realize firsthand the power of God the Creator.

In the Seventh Message, "People Will Get Up, Leap, and Walk," the story of a paralytic who comes before

Jesus with the help of his friends, gets up, and walks, is carefully examined. Moreover, the Message also enlightens the readers on the kinds of deeds of faith they are to present before God in order to experience such power today.

The Eighth Message, "People Will Rejoice, Dance, and Sing," delves into the story of a deaf mute who receives healing when he comes before Jesus, and introduces the ways in which we can also experience such power even today.

Finally, in the Ninth Message, "The Unfailing Providence of God," prophecies on the last days and the providence of God for Manmin Joong-ang Church – both of which have been revealed by God Himself since the founding of Manmin more than twenty years ago – are explained plainly.

Through this work, may countless people come to possess true faith, always experience the power of God the Creator, and be utilized as vessels of the Holy Spirit and accomplish His providence, in the name of our Lord Jesus Christ I pray!

Geumsun Vin,
Director of Editorial Bureau

CONTENTS

Message 1

To Believe in God

Hebrews 11:3

By faith
we understand that
the universe was formed
at God's command,
so that what is seen
was not made out of
what was visible.

Hallelujah! I give all thanks and glory to our Father God who has blessed us to conduct the 11th Two-week Special Revival Meeting.

Since the first annual Two-week Special Revival Meeting held in May 1993, countless people have had firsthand experiences of the ever-increasing power and the work of God, by which diseases that could not be healed by modern medicine were healed and problems that could not be solved by science were solved. For the last 11 years, as we find in Mark 16:20, God has confirmed His word by the signs that accompanied it.

Through the messages of great depths on faith, righteousness, flesh and spirit, good and light, love, and the like, God has led a number of Manmin members to the deeper spiritual realm. Furthermore, through each Revival Meeting, God has led us to witness His power firsthand so that it has now become a world-renowned Revival Meeting.

Jesus tells us in Mark 9:23, *"'If you can?' Everything is possible for him who believes."* Therefore, if we possess true faith, nothing is impossible for us and we will receive whatever we seek.

What, then, are we to believe and how are we to

believe it? If we do not know and believe God correctly, we would not be able to experience His power and it would be difficult to receive answers from Him. That is why understanding and believing correctly is of the utmost importance.

Who is God?

First, God is the author of the sixty-six books of the Bible. 2 Timothy 3:16 reminds us that *"All Scripture is God-breathed."* The Bible consists of sixty-six books and is estimated to have been recorded by thirty-four different people over the span of 1,600 years. Yet, the most amazing aspect of each book of the Bible is that, despite the fact that it was recorded by many different people over many centuries, from the beginning to the end it is congruent and corresponding to each other. In other words, the Bible is the Word of God recorded in inspiration by different people He deemed fit from different periods of history, and through it He reveals Himself. That is why those who believe the Bible to be the Word of God and obey it can experience blessings and grace He has promised.

Next, God is "I Am Who I Am" (Exodus 3:14). Unlike

idols created by man's imagination or carved by his hand, our God is the true God who has existed from before the eternity to the eternity. Furthermore, we can describe God as love (1 John 4:16), light (1 John 1:5), and the judge of all things at the end of the time. Yet, above all else, we must remember that God, with His astounding power, created all things of the heavens and the earth. He is the Almighty One who has steadfastly manifested His wondrous power from the time of the Creation to this day.

The Creator of All Things

In Genesis 1:1, we find that *"In the beginning God created the heavens and the earth."* Hebrews 11:3 tells us, *"By faith we understand that the universe was formed at God's command, so that what is seen was not made out of what was visible."*

In the state of vacuity at the beginning of time, by God's power everything in the universe was created. By His power, God created the sun and the moon in the sky, plants and trees, birds and animals, fish in the sea, and mankind.

Despite this fact, many people are unable to believe in God the Creator because the concept of creation is simply too contradictory to the knowledge or experience they have gained and had in the world. For instance, in the mind of such people, it is not possible for all things in the universe to have been created at God's command from the state of vacuity.

This is why the theory of evolution was conceived. Adherers to the evolution theory argue that a living organism came into existence by chance, evolved on its own, and multiplied. If people deny God's creation of the universe with such a frame of knowledge, they are unable to believe the rest of the Bible. They are unable to believe in preaching of the existence of heaven and hell because they have never been there, and in proclaiming of the Son of God who was born a man, died, resurrected, and ascended into heaven.

However, we find that as science advances, the fallacy of evolution is exposed while the legitimacy of creation continues to gain ground. Even if we do not produce a list of scientific evidences, there are myriads of examples that testify to the creation.

Evidences of God the Creator

Here is one such example. There are over two hundred

countries and even more different ethnic groups of people. Yet, whether they are white, black, or yellow, each of them has two eyes. Each of them has two ears, one nose, and two nostrils. This pattern applies not only to human beings but also to animals on the ground, birds in the sky, and fish in the sea. Just because the trunk of an elephant is exceptionally large and long, that does not mean that it has more than two nostrils. Each of the human beings, animals, birds, and fish has one mouth, and the position at which the mouth is placed is identical. There are subtle differences with respect to the position of each organ among different species, but for the most part the structure and position are indistinguishable.

How could all of this have taken place "by chance"? This is a piece of solid evidence that one Creator designed and formed the countless people, animals, birds, and fish. If there had been more than one creator, the appearance and structure of living things would have been as different as the number and preferences of the creators. However, because our God is the only Creator, all living things were formed according to the identical design.

Furthermore, we can find countless more evidences in the nature and the universe, all of which lead us to believe in God's having created everything. As Romans 1:20 tells us, *"For since the creation of the world God's invisible qualities – his eternal power and divine nature – have been clearly seen, being understood from what has been made, so that men are without excuse,"* God designed and formed all things so that the truth of His existence cannot be denied or refuted.

In Habakkuk 2:18-19, God tells us, *"Of what value is an idol, since a man has carved it? Or an image that teaches lies? For he who makes it trusts in his own creation; he makes idols that cannot speak. Woe to him who says to wood, 'Come to life!' Or to lifeless stone, 'Wake up!' Can it give guidance? It is covered with gold and silver; there is no breath in it."* If any of you has served or believed in idols without having known God, you must thoroughly repent of your sins by rending your hearts.

Biblical Evidences by which We Can Certainly Believe in God the Creator

There are still many people who are unable to believe in God despite an immeasurable number of evidences around them. That is why, by manifesting His power, God has shown us more apparent and undeniable evidences of

His existence. With miracles that cannot be produced by man, God has allowed mankind to believe in His existence and wondrous work.

In the Bible, there are many fascinating instances in which God's power was manifested. The Red Sea was split, the sun stood still or it went backward, and the fire from heaven was brought down. Bitter water in the wilderness turned into sweet, drinkable water while from a rock sprang out water. The dead revived, diseases were healed, and seemingly lost battles were won.

When people believe in the almighty God and ask Him, they can experience the unimaginable work of His power. That is why God recorded in the Bible many instances in which His power was manifested and blesses us to believe.

Yet, the work of His power does not exist in the Bible alone. Because God is unchanging, through countless signs, wonders, and work of His power, He is manifesting His power through true believers all over the world today; He promised us so. In Mark 9:23, Jesus reassures us, *"'If you can?' Everything is possible for him who believes."* In Mark 16:17-18, our Lord reminds us, *"And these signs will accompany those who believe: In my name they will drive out demons; they will speak in new tongues; they will pick up snakes with their hands; and when they drink deadly poison, it will not hurt them at all; they will place their hands on sick people, and they will get well."*

The power of God manifested at Manmin Joong-ang Church

The church at which I serve as senior pastor, Manmin Joong-ang Church, has manifested the work of the power of God the Creator time and again as it has been striving to spread the gospel to the ends of the world. Since the founding in 1982 to this day, Manmin has led countless people to the way of salvation with the power of God the Creator. The most notable work of His power is the healing of diseases and infirmities. Many people with "incurable" diseases including cancer, tuberculosis, paralysis, cerebral palsy, hernia, arthritis, leukemia, and the like have been healed. Demons were driven out, the lame stood up and began walking and running, and those who had been paralyzed from various accidents became well. In addition, immediately after receiving prayer, people who had suffered from severe burns were healed without any ghastly scars remaining. Others whose bodies had become stiffened and who had already lost consciousness from brain hemorrhage or gas poisoning

"How grateful I was
when you saved my life
I thought I would rely on my crutches
for the rest of my life.

Now, I can walk...
Father, Father I thank You!"

Deaconess Heejin Park, who was to be permanently handicapped, throws away and walks after receiving prayer

revived and recovered right away. Still others who had stopped breathing came back to life after receiving prayer.

Many others, who had not been able to have children after five, seven, ten, even twenty years of marriage, received blessings of conceiving after receiving prayer. Countless individuals who had not been able to hear, see, and speak greatly glorified God after recovering those abilities with prayer.

Even if science and medicine have made giant leaps year after year, century after century, dead nerves cannot be revived and innate blindness or deafness cannot be healed. However, the almighty God is able to do anything, as He creates something out of nothing.

I experienced the power of the almighty God myself. I had been at the threshold of death for seven years before I came to believe in Him. I was ill in all parts of my body, with the exception of my two eyes, that I was nicknamed the "disease department store." In vain I tried Eastern and Western medicine, lepers' medicine, all kinds of herbs, gallbladders of bears and dogs, centipedes, and even excremental water. I made every effort during those agonizing seven years, but could not be healed. When I was in great despair in the spring of 1974, I had an unbelievable experience. At the moment I met God, He

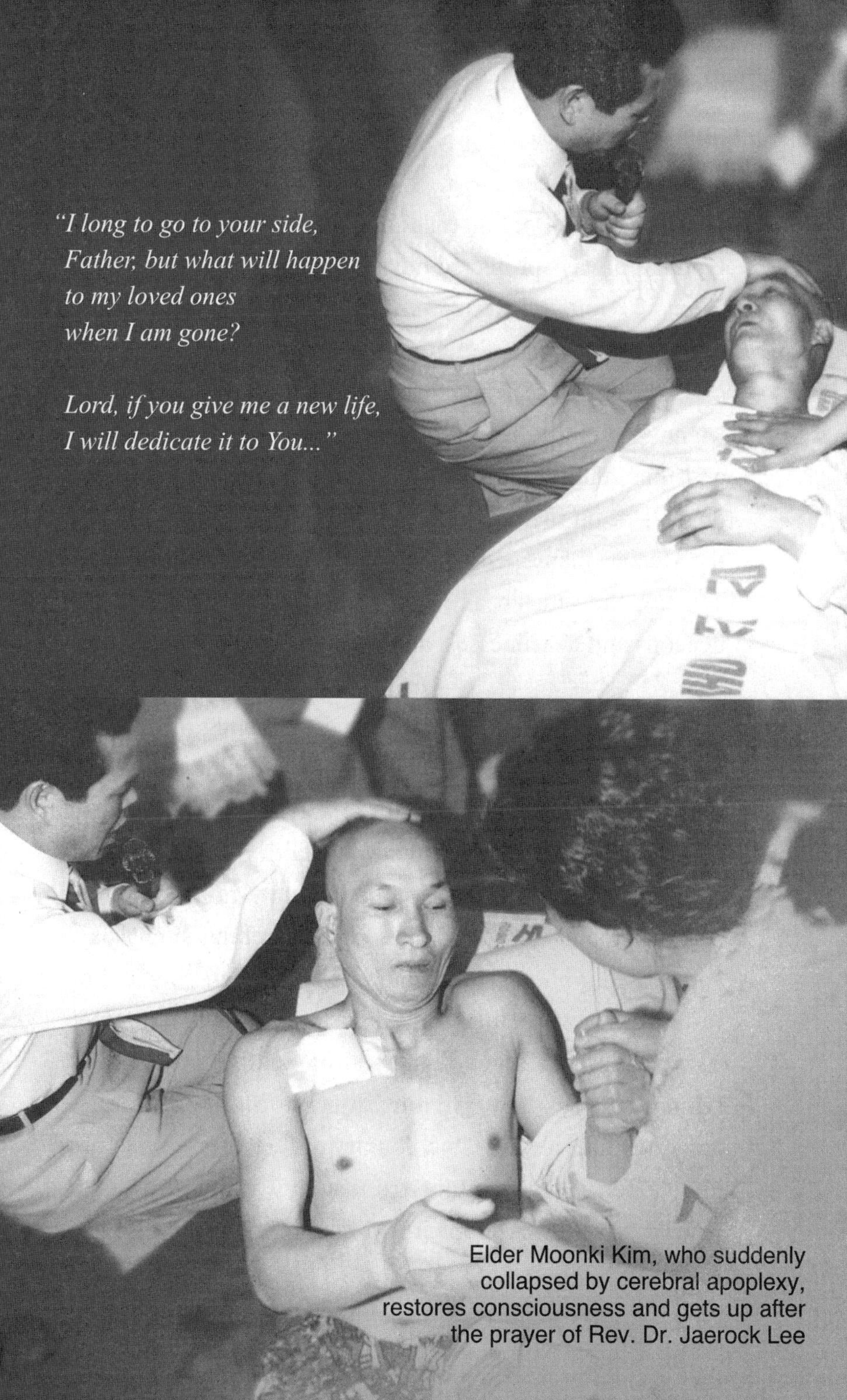

"I long to go to your side,
Father, but what will happen
to my loved ones
when I am gone?

Lord, if you give me a new life,
I will dedicate it to You..."

Elder Moonki Kim, who suddenly collapsed by cerebral apoplexy, restores consciousness and gets up after the prayer of Rev. Dr. Jaerock Lee healed me of all my diseases and infirmities. Thenceforth, God has always protected me so that I have never been ill. Even if I felt a little uncomfortable in any parts of my body, after prayer with faith I was immediately healed.

Besides myself and my family, I know that many Manmin members believe sincerely in the almighty God and thus, they are always physically healthy and are not dependent on medicine. In gratitude of the mercy of God the Healer, many people who have become well are now serving the church as loyal ministers of God, elders, deacons and deaconesses, and workers.

The power of God is not limited to healing of diseases and infirmities. Since the church was founded in 1982, many Manmin members have witnessed countless instances in which prayer with the faith in God's power controls the weather as it stopped heavy rains, shielded Manmin members with clouds on a scorching sunny day, and caused typhoons to die out or change their course. For instance, in every July and August church-wide summer retreats are held. Even if the rest of South Korea suffers from damages brought on by typhoons and floods, locations and parts of the country where the retreats are held often remain intact from heavy rains and other natural disasters. A number of Manmin members also see rainbows on a regular basis, even on days when it has not rained earlier.

There is even a more amazing aspect of God's power. The work of His power is manifested even when I do not directly pray for sick people. Countless people have greatly glorified God after receiving healing and blessings through the "Prayer for the Sick" for the entire congregation from the pulpit, and the "Prayer" recorded on cassette tapes, Internet broadcasts, and automated telephone messages.

Furthermore, in Acts 19:12 we find *"that [when] handkerchiefs and aprons that had touched [the apostle Paul] were taken to the sick, their illnesses were cured and the evil spirits left them."* Likewise, through the handkerchiefs on which I prayed, the work of God's wondrous power is manifested.

Moreover, when I lay my hands on and pray on the photographs of the sick, healings that transcend time and space take place all over the world. This is why, when I conduct an overseas crusade, all kinds of diseases and infirmities, including the deadly AIDS, are healed in an instant by the power of God that transcends time and space.

To Experience the Power of God

Does this mean that anyone who believes in God can experience the astounding work of His power and receive answers and blessings? Many people profess their faith in God, but not all of them experience the power. You can experience His power only when your faith in God is exhibited in deed and He acknowledges, "I know you believe in me."

God will consider the mere fact that one listens to somebody's preaching and comes to attend a worship service as "faith." However, in order to possess true faith by which you can receive healing and answers, you must hear and know about who God is, about why Jesus is our Savior, and of the existence of heaven and hell. When you understand these factors, repent of your sins, accept Jesus as your Savior, and receive the Holy Spirit, you will receive a right as a child of God. This is the first step towards true faith.

People who possess true faith will show deeds that testify to such faith. God will see the deeds of faith and answer to the desires of their hearts. Those who experience the work of His power demonstrate the evidences of faith to Him and are approved by God.

Pleasing God with Deeds of Faith

Here are a few examples from the Bible. First, in 2 Kings 5 is the story of Naaman, commander of the army of the king of Aram. Naaman experienced the work of God's power after demonstrating deeds of his faith by obeying Prophet Elisha, through whom God spoke.

Naaman was a distinguished general of the kingdom of Aram. When he had leprosy Naaman visited Elisha, who was said to perform miraculous wonders. However, when such an influential and renowned general as Naaman arrived at Elisha's with a great quantity of gold, silver, and clothing, the prophet merely sent a messenger to Naaman, and told him, "Go, wash yourself seven times in the Jordan."

At first, Naaman was visibly angry largely because he did not receive proper treatment from the prophet. In addition, instead of Elisha's praying for him, Naaman was told to go wash himself in the Jordan River. However, Naaman soon changed his mind and obeyed. Even though the words of Elisha were not to his liking and did not agree with his thoughts, Naaman was determined to at least try obeying a prophet of God.

By the time Naaman washed himself six times in the Jordan River, no visible changes had been made to his leprosy. Yet, when Naaman washed himself in the Jordan a seventh time, his flesh was restored and became clean like that of a young boy.

Spiritually, "water" symbolizes the Word of God. The fact that Naaman "dipped himself" in the Jordan River means that by His Word, Naaman was cleansed of his sins. Furthermore, the number "7" signifies perfection; the fact that Naaman dipped himself in the River "seven times" means that the general received complete forgiveness.

By the same token, if we desire to receive God's answers, we must first thoroughly repent of all our sins, the way Naaman did. Yet, repentance does not end with merely saying, "I repent. I have done wrong." You ought to "rend your heart" (Joel 2:13). Furthermore, when you thoroughly repent of your sins, you must resolve never to commit the same sin again. Only then will the wall of sin between you and God be destroyed, happiness spring from within, your problems be solved, and you receive answers to desires of your heart.

Second, in 1 Kings 3 we find King Solomon offering a thousand burnt offerings before God. Through these offerings, Solomon demonstrated deeds of his faith in order to receive God's answers, and as a consequence received from God not only what he had asked, but also what he had not asked.

For Solomon to offer a thousand burnt offerings, it required a great amount of dedication. For each offering, the king would have had to capture animals and prepare them. Can you imagine how much time, effort, and money it would have cost to give such offerings a thousand times? The kind of devotion Solomon demonstrated would not have been possible if the king had not believed in the living God.

When He saw Solomon's dedication, God gave him not only wisdom, which the king had originally sought, but also riches and honor – so that in his lifetime he had no equal among kings.

Lastly, in Matthew 15 is the story of a woman from Syrian Phoenicia whose daughter was demon-possessed. She came before Jesus in a humble and unchanging heart, asked Jesus for healing, and received the desire of her heart in the end. However, at the earnest begging of the woman, Jesus did not initially respond, "All right, your daughter is healed." Instead, He said to the woman, "It is not right to take the children's bread and toss it to their dogs." He compared the woman to a dog. If the woman had been without faith, she would have been either horribly embarrassed or uncontrollably angry. Yet, this woman had the faith that assured her of Jesus' answer, and was neither disappointed nor dismayed. Instead, she clung to Jesus even more humbly. "Yes, Lord," the woman told Jesus, "but even the dogs eat the crumbs that fall from their masters' table." At this, Jesus was greatly delighted by the woman's faith and immediately healed her demon-possessed daughter.

Similarly, if we want to receive healing and answers, we must demonstrate our faith to the end. Moreover, if you possess faith by which you can receive His answers, you must physically present yourself before God.

Of course, because God's power is manifested greatly at Manmin Joong-ang Church, it is possible to receive healing with the handkerchief on which I prayed or with photographs. However, unless the one who is ill is in a critical condition or abroad, the person himself must come before God. One can experience the power of God only after hearing His Word and possessing faith.

If the person is mentally retarded or demon-possessed and thus cannot come before God by his own faith, then like the woman from Syrian Phoenicia, his parents or family must come before God on his behalf in love and faith.

In addition to these, there are many more evidences of faith. For instance, in the face of an individual who possesses faith by which he can receive answers, happiness and gratitude are always evident. In Mark 11:24, Jesus tells us, *"Therefore I tell you, whatever you ask for in prayer, believe that you have received, and it will be yours."* If you have true faith, you can only be glad and grateful at all times. Additionally, if you profess to believe in God, you will obey and live by His Word. Since God is light, you will strive to walk in the light and transform.

God delights in our deeds of faith and answers the desires of our hearts. Do you possess the kind and measure of faith of which God will approve?

In Hebrews 11:6 we are reminded, *"And without faith it is impossible to please God, because anyone who comes to him must believe that he exists and that he rewards those who earnestly seek him."*

By properly understanding what it is to believe in God and demonstrating your faith, may each of you please Him, experience His power, and lead a blessed life, in the name of our Lord Jesus Christ I pray!

Message 2

To Believe in the Lord

Hebrews 12:1-2

Therefore, since we are surrounded
by such a great cloud of witnesses,
let us throw off everything that hinders
and the sin that so easily entangles,
and let us run with perseverance
the race marked out for us.
Let us fix our eyes on Jesus,
the author and perfecter of our faith,
who for the joy set before him endured the cross,
scorning its shame, and sat down
at the right hand of the throne of God.

Many people today have heard the name "Jesus Christ." A surprising number of people, however, do not know why Jesus is the only Savior for mankind or why we receive salvation only when we believe in Jesus Christ. Much worse, there are some Christians who are unable to answer the questions above, even though they are directly related with salvation. This means that these Christians are leading their lives in Christ without fully understanding the spiritual significance of those questions.

Therefore, only when we correctly know and understand why Jesus is our only Savior and what it is to accept and believe in Him, and possess true faith, can we experience the power of God.

Some people simply consider Jesus as one of the four great saints. Others merely think of Him as the founder of Christianity, or as a very magnanimous man who did a great deal of good during His life.

However, those of us who have become children of God must be able to confess that Jesus is the Savior of mankind who redeemed all people from their sins. How can we possibly compare the only Son of God, Jesus Christ, to human beings, mere creatures? Even in Jesus' time, we find that there were many diverse perspectives through which people thought of Him.

The Son of God the Creator Comes as the Savior

In Matthew 16 is a scene in which Jesus asked His disciples, "Who do people say the Son of Man is?" In quoting different people's responses, the disciples answered, "Some say John the Baptist; others say Elijah; and still others, Jeremiah or one of the prophets." Then Jesus asked His disciples, "Who do you say I am?" When Peter answered, "You are the Christ, the Son of the living God," Jesus commended him, "Blessed are you, Simon son of Jonah, for this was not revealed to you by man, but by my Father in heaven." Through countless works of God's power Jesus manifested, Peter was certain that He was the Son of God the Creator and the Christ, the Savior of mankind.

In the beginning, God created a man from the dust in His own image, and led him to the Garden of Eden. In the Garden were the tree of life and the tree of the knowledge of good and evil, and God commanded the first man Adam, *"You are free to eat from any tree in the garden; but you must not eat from the tree of the knowledge of good and evil, for when you eat of it you will surely die"* (Genesis 2:16-17).

After a long time had passed, the first man and woman Adam and Eve were tempted by the serpent, which was incited by Satan, and disobeyed God's command. In the end, they ate from the tree of the knowledge of good and evil and were driven out from the Garden of Eden. As a consequence of their deeds, descendants of Adam and Eve inherited their sinful nature. Moreover, as God had told Adam he would surely die, all the spirits of his descendants were led to eternal death.

Therefore, before the beginning of time, God prepared the way of salvation, the Son of God the Creator Jesus Christ. As Acts 4:12 tells us, *"Salvation is found in no one else, for there is no other name under heaven given to men by which we must be saved,"* except for Jesus Christ, no one else in the history is qualified to be the Savior of mankind.

The Providence of God that Had Been Hidden Before Time Began

1 Corinthians 2:6-7 tell us, *"We do, however, speak a message of wisdom among the mature, but not the wisdom*

of this age or of the rulers of this age, who are coming to nothing. No, we speak of God's secret wisdom, a wisdom that has been hidden and that God destined for our glory before time began." 1 Corinthians 2:8-9 continue to remind us, *"None of the rulers of this age understood it, for if they had, they would not have crucified the Lord of glory. However, as it is written: 'No eye has seen, no ear has heard, no mind has conceived what God has prepared for those who love him.'"* We must realize that the way to salvation God prepared for mankind before the beginning of time is the way of the cross by Jesus Christ, and this is God's wisdom that has been hidden.

As the Creator, God always rules everything in the universe and governs the history of mankind. The king or the president of a country governs his country according to the law of the land; the chief executive officer of a corporation oversees his company according to the company guidelines; and the head of a household supervises his family according to family rules. Likewise, even though God is the owner of all things in the universe, He always governs all things according to the law of the spiritual realm as found in the Bible.

According to the law of the spiritual realm, there is a rule, *"The wages of sin is death"* (Romans 6:23), which punishes the guilty, and there is also a rule that can redeem us from our sins. That is why God applied the rule to redeem us from our sins in order to restore the authority that had been lost to the enemy devil with Adam's disobedience.

What was the rule by which mankind could be redeemed and restore the authority the first man Adam relinquished to the enemy devil? According to the "law on the redemption of the land," God prepared the way of salvation for mankind before time began.

Jesus Christ is Qualified according to the Law on the Redemption of the Land

God gave the Israelites the "law on the redemption of the land," which dictated the following: the land was not to be sold permanently; and, if one became poor and sold his land, his nearest relative or the person himself was to come and redeem the land, thereby restoring the ownership of the land (Leviticus 25:23-28).

God knew in advance that Adam would relinquish the authority he received from God to the devil by his disobedience. Furthermore, as the true and original Owner of all things in the universe, God handed over to the devil the authority and glory Adam had once possessed, as was required by the law of the spiritual realm. That is why when the devil tempted Jesus in Luke 4:5-7 by showing Him all the kingdoms of the world, he could tell Jesus, *"I will give you all their authority and splendor, for it has been given to me, and I can give it to anyone I want to."*

According to the law on the redemption of the land, all lands belong to God. Thus, man can never sell them permanently and when an individual with proper qualifications appears, the sold lands must be restored to that person. Likewise, all things in the universe belong to God, so Adam could not "sell" them permanently, and neither could the devil own them permanently. Therefore, when an individual able enough to redeem Adam's lost authority appeared, the enemy devil had no choice but to surrender the authority he had received from Adam.

Before the beginning of time, the God of justice prepared a blameless man qualified according to the law on the redemption of the land, and that way of salvation for mankind is Jesus Christ.

How, then, according to the law on the redemption of the land, could Jesus Christ restore the authority that had been handed over to the enemy devil? Only when Jesus met the following four qualifications, could He redeem all men from sins and restore the authority that had been handed over to the enemy devil.

First, the redeemer must be a man, Adam's "nearest relative."

Leviticus 25:25 tells us, *"If one of your countrymen becomes poor and sells some of his property, his nearest relative is to come and redeem what his countryman had sold."* Since "the nearest relative" could redeem the land, in order to restore the authority Adam had relinquished, that "nearest relative" must be a man. 1 Corinthians 15:21-22 read, *"For since death came through a man, the resurrection of the dead comes also through a man. For as in Adam all die, so in Christ all will be made alive."* In other words, as death entered through the disobedience of one man, the resurrection of the dead spirit must be accomplished through one man.

Jesus Christ is "the Word [that] became flesh" and came to the earth (John 1:14). He is the Son of God, born in flesh with both of divine and human nature. Moreover, His birth is a historical fact and there are many evidences that testify to this fact. Most notably, the history of mankind is denoted using "B.C." or *"Before Christ,"* and "A.D." or *"Anno Domini"* in Latin, which means "in the year of our Lord."

Since Jesus Christ entered the world in flesh, He is the "nearest relative" of Adam and meets the first qualification.

Second, the redeemer must not be a descendant of Adam.

For an individual to redeem others from their sins, he must not be a sinner himself. All descendants of Adam, who himself became a sinner through his disobedience, are sinners. Therefore, according to the law on the redemption of the land, the redeemer must not be a descendant of Adam.

In Revelation 5:1-3 is the following:

> *Then I saw in the right hand of him who sat on the throne a scroll with writing on both sides and sealed with seven seals. And I saw a mighty angel proclaiming in a loud voice, 'Who is worthy to break the seals and open the scroll?' But no one in heaven or on earth or under the earth could open the scroll or even look inside it.*

Here, the scroll "sealed with seven seals" refers to a contract forged between God and the devil after Adam's disobedience, and the one who is "worthy to break the seals and open the scroll" must be qualified according to the law on the redemption of the land. When the apostle John looked around for the one who could break the seals and open the scroll, he could not find any.

John looked up in heaven and there were angels but no men. He looked on earth and only saw Adam's descendants, all sinners. He looked under the earth and only saw sinners destined to hell and beings that belong to the devil. John wept and wept because no one was found who was qualified according to the law on the redemption of the land (v. 4).

Then, one of the elders comforted John, and told him *"Do not weep! See, the Lion of the tribe of Judah, the Root of David, has triumphed. He is able to open the scroll and its seven seals."* Here, "the Lion of the tribe of Judah, the Root of David" refers to Jesus, who is of the tribe of Judah and of the house of David; Jesus Christ is qualified to be the redeemer according to the law on the redemption of the land.

From Matthew 1:18-21, we find a detailed account of the birth of our Lord:

> *This is how the birth of Jesus Christ came about: His mother Mary was pledged to be married to*

> *Joseph, but before they came together, she was found to be with child through the Holy Spirit. Because Joseph her husband was a righteous man and did not want to expose her to public disgrace, he had in mind to divorce her quietly. But after he had considered this, an angel of the Lord appeared to him in a dream and said, "Joseph son of David, do not be afraid to take Mary home as your wife, because what is conceived in her is from the Holy Spirit. She will give birth to a son, and you are to give him the name Jesus, because he will save his people from their sins.*

The reason God's only Son Jesus Christ came into this world as flesh (John 1:14) through the womb of the Virgin Mary is because Jesus had to be a man but not a descendant of Adam, so that He could be qualified according to the law on the redemption of the land.

Third, the redeemer must have power.

Suppose a younger brother becomes poor and sells his land, and his older brother wants to redeem the land for his younger brother. Then, the older brother must acquire sufficient means to redeem it (Leviticus 25:26). Similarly, if the younger brother is in great debt and his older brother wants to pay back the debt, the older brother can do so when he has "sufficient means," not just good intention.

By the same token, in order to transform a sinner into a righteous man, "sufficient means" or power is necessary. Here, the power to redeem the land refers to the power to redeem all men from sins. In other words, the redeemer of all men who is qualified according to the law on the redemption of the land cannot have any sins found in him.

Since Jesus Christ is not a descendant of Adam, He has no original sin. Neither does Jesus Christ have any self-committed sins since He kept all the law during His 33 years of life on the earth. He was circumcised on the eighth day after His birth and prior to His three-year ministry, Jesus fully obeyed and loved His parents to the utmost, and devotedly kept all the commandments.

That is why Hebrews 7:26 tells us, *"Such a high priest meets our need – one who is holy, blameless, pure, set apart from sinners, exalted above the heavens."* In 1 Peter 2:22-23, we find, *"He committed no sin, and no deceit was found in his mouth. When they hurled their insults at him, he did not retaliate; when he suffered, he made no threats. Instead, he entrusted himself to him who judges justly."*

Fourth, the redeemer must have love.

In order for the redemption of the land to be fulfilled, in addition to the three conditions above, love is required. Without love, an older brother who is able to redeem the land for his younger brother will not redeem the land. Even if an older brother is the richest man in the land while his younger brother has an astronomical amount of debt, without love the older brother would not help the younger brother. What good would the older brother's power and wealth do for the younger brother?

In Ruth 4 is the story of Boaz, who was well aware of the condition in which Ruth's mother-in-law Naomi found herself. When Boaz asked the "kinsman-redeemer" to redeem Naomi's inheritance, the kinsman-redeemer responded, "Then I cannot redeem it because I might endanger my own estate. You redeem it yourself. I cannot do it" (v. 6). Then Boaz, in his abundant love, redeemed the land for Naomi. Afterwards, Boaz was greatly blessed to be an ancestor of David.

Jesus, who came into the world in flesh, was not a descendant of Adam because He was conceived by the Holy Spirit, and committed no sin. Hence, He had "sufficient means" to redeem us. If Jesus had had no love, however, He would not have endured the agony of the crucifixion. Yet, Jesus was so full of love that He was crucified by mere creatures, shed all His blood, and redeemed mankind, thereby opening the way of salvation. This is the result of the immeasurable love of our Father God and the sacrifice of Jesus who was obedient to the point of death.

The Reason Jesus was Hung on a Tree

Why was Jesus hung on a wooden cross? This is to satisfy the law of the spiritual realm, which dictates that *"Christ redeemed us from the curse of the law by becoming a curse for us, for it is written: 'Cursed is everyone who is hung on a tree'"* (Galatians 3:13). Jesus was hung on a tree on our behalf so that He could redeem us sinners from "the curse of the law."

Leviticus 17:11 tells us, *"For the life of a creature is in the blood, and I have given it to you to make atonement for yourselves on the altar; it is the blood that makes atonement for one's life."* Hebrews 9:22 reads, *"In fact, the law requires that nearly everything be cleansed with blood, and without the shedding of blood there is no forgiveness."* Blood is life because there is no forgiveness without the shedding of blood. Jesus shed His blameless and precious blood so that we would gain life.

Furthermore, through His suffering on the cross, believers are set free from the curse of diseases, infirmities, poverty, and the like. Since Jesus lived in poverty while on the earth, He took care of our poverty. Since Jesus was flogged, we are free from all our diseases. Since Jesus wore the crown of thorns, He redeemed us from the sins we commit with our thoughts. Since Jesus was nailed through His hands and feet, He redeemed us from all our sins we commit with our hands and feet.

To Believe in the Lord is to Change into the Truth

People who truly understand the providence of the cross and believe it from the depths of their hearts will rid themselves of sins and live by the will of God. As Jesus tells us in John 14:23, *"If anyone loves me, he will obey my teaching. My Father will love him, and we will come to him and make our home with him,"* such individuals will receive God's love and blessings.

Why, then, do people who confess their faith in the Lord not receive answers to their prayer and live in the midst of trials and afflictions? That is because, even if they may say that they believe in God, God does not consider their faith as true faith. This means that despite having heard the Word of God, they have not yet ridden themselves of their sins and changed into the truth.

For instance, there are countless believers who fail to obey the Ten Commandments, the fundamentals of life in Christ. Such individuals are aware of the command "Remember the Sabbath day, and keep it holy." Yet, they only attend the morning service or not attend any services at all and do their own work on Sundays. They know they are to give tithes, but because money is too dear to them they fail to give the whole tithes. When God specifically told us that failure to give whole tithes is "robbing" Him, how would they receive answers and blessings (Malachi 3:8)?

Then there are those believers who do not forgive mistakes and faults of others. They become angry and devise plans to pay back to the same degree of evil. Some make promises but break them time and again, while others blame and lament, exactly as the worldly people do. How could they be said to possess true faith?

If we have true faith, we must strive to do all things according to the will of God, avoid every kind of evil, and resemble our Lord who has surrendered His own life for us sinners. Such people can forgive and love those who hate and hurt them, and always serve and sacrifice themselves for others.

When you rid yourself of hot-temperedness, you will be transformed into a kind person whose lips will only utter words of goodness and warmth. If you complained on every occasion before, by true faith you will turn to give thanks in all circumstances and share grace to all those around you.

If we truly believe in the Lord, each of us must resemble Him and lead a transformed life. This is the way to receive God's answers and blessings.

Hebrews 12:1-2 tell us:

> *Therefore, since we are surrounded by such a great cloud of witnesses, let us throw off everything that hinders and the sin that so easily entangles, and let us run with perseverance the race marked out for us. Let us fix our eyes on Jesus, the author and perfecter of our faith, who for the joy set before him endured the cross, scorning its shame, and sat down at the right hand of the throne of God.*

Aside from many forefathers of faith we find in the Bible, among those around us, there are many people who have received salvation and blessings by their faith in our Lord.

Like "a great cloud of witnesses," let us possess true faith! Let us throw off everything that hinders and the sin that so easily entangles, and strive to resemble our Lord! Only then, as Jesus promises us in John 15:7, *"If you remain in me and my words remain in you, ask whatever you wish, and it will be given to you,"* will each of us lead a life which is filled with His answers and blessings.

If you are not yet leading such a life, look back at your life, rend your heart and repent for not having correctly believed in the Lord, and resolve to live only by the Word of God.

May each of you possess true faith, experience God's power, and greatly glorify Him with all your answers and blessings, in the name of our Lord Jesus Christ I pray!

Message 3

A Vessel More Beautiful than a Jewel

2 Timothy 2:20-21 (King James Version)

But in a great house
there are not only vessels of gold
and silver, but also of wood and earth;
and some to honour;
some to dishonour.
If a man therefore purge himself from these,
he shall be a vessel unto honour,
sanctified, and meet for the master's use,
and prepared unto every good work.

God created mankind so that He could reap true children with whom He could share true love. Yet, people sinned, going astray from the true purpose of their creation, and became slaves of the enemy devil and Satan (Romans 3:23). The God of love, however, did not give up the goal of reaping true children. He opened the way of salvation for people found in the midst of sin. God had His one and only Son Jesus crucified on a cross so that He could redeem all men from sins.

By this amazing love accompanied by great sacrifice, for anyone who believes in Jesus Christ the way of salvation has been opened. To anyone who believes in his heart that Jesus died and rose again from the grave and confesses with his lips that Jesus is his Savior, the right as a child of God is given.

God's Beloved Children Likened to "Vessels"

As 2 Timothy 2:20-21 read, *"But in a great house there are not only vessels of gold and silver, but also of wood and earth; and some to honour; some to dishonour. If a man therefore purge himself from these, he shall be a vessel unto honour, sanctified, and meet for the master's use, and prepared unto every good work" (King James Version),* the purpose of a vessel is to contain objects. God likens His children to "vessels" because in them He can fill His love and grace, and His Word that is the truth, as well as His power and authority. Therefore, we must realize that depending on the kinds of vessels we prepare, we can enjoy all kinds of good gifts and blessings God has prepared for us.

What kind of vessel, then, is an individual who can contain all the blessings God has prepared? It is a vessel which God deems precious, noble, and beautiful.

First, a "precious" vessel is the one who wholly fulfills his God-given duty. John the Baptist who prepared the way for our Lord Jesus, and Moses who led the Israelites out of Egypt belong to this category.

Next, a "noble" vessel is the one with such qualities as honesty, truthfulness, resolution, and fidelity, all of which are rare in ordinary people. Joseph and Daniel, both of whom held position equivalent of prime minister of powerful countries and greatly glorified God, belong to this category.

Last, a "beautiful" vessel before God is the one with a good heart who never quarrels or bickers but in the truth accepts and tolerates all things. Esther who saved her countrymen and Abraham who was called God's "friend" belong to this category.

"A vessel more beautiful than a jewel" is an individual who possesses qualifications to be regarded precious, noble, and beautiful by God. A jewel hidden amongst gravels is immediately noticeable. Likewise, all God's people who are more beautiful than jewels are without doubt noticeable.

Most jewels are costly for their size, but the glitters and their various yet distinctive colors attract people in the pursuit of beauty. However, not all glittery stones are considered jewels. Genuine jewels must also possess hues and luster, as well as physical solidity. Here, "physical solidity" refers to a material's ability to withstand heat, not be contaminated by the contact with other substances, and maintain its shape. Another important factor is scarcity.

If there is a vessel of magnificent brilliance, physical solidity, and scarcity, how precious, noble, and beautiful would this vessel be? God wants His children to become vessels more beautiful than jewels and wants them to lead blessed lives. When God discovers such vessels, He abundantly pours into them the signs of His love and delight.

How can we become vessels more beautiful than jewels in the sight of God?

First, you must accomplish sanctification of your heart with the Word of God, which is the truth itself.

In order for a vessel to be used according to its original purpose, above all it must be clean. Even an expensive, golden vessel cannot be used if it is stained and marked with stench. Only when this expensive, golden vessel is cleansed in water can it be used according to its purpose.

The same rule applies to the children of God. For His children, God has prepared abundant blessings and a variety of gifts, blessings of riches and health, and the like. In order for us to receive those blessings and gifts, we must first prepare ourselves as clean vessels.

We find in Jeremiah 17:9, *"The heart is deceitful above all things and beyond cure. Who can understand it?"* We also find in Matthew 15:18-19, in which Jesus says, *"But the things that come out of the mouth come from the heart, and these make a man 'unclean.' For out of the heart come evil thoughts, murder, adultery, sexual immorality, theft, false testimony, slander."* Therefore, only after we cleanse our hearts can we become clean vessels. Once a clean vessel, none of us will ever think "evil thoughts," utter evil words, or carry out evil deeds.

The cleansing of our hearts is possible only with spiritual water, the Word of God. That is why the Bible urges each believer to make him holy, cleansing him by the washing with water through the word (Ephesians 5:26), and encourages each of us to draw near to God with a sincere heart in full assurance of faith, having our hearts sprinkled to cleanse us from a guilty conscience and having our bodies washed with pure water (Hebrews 10:22).

How, then, does spiritual water – the Word of God – cleanse us? We must obey a variety of commands found in the sixty-six books of the Bible that serve to "cleanse" our hearts. Obeying such commands as "Do not's" and "Cast away's" will ultimately lead us to rid ourselves of all that is sinful and evil.

The behavior of those who have cleansed their hearts with His Word will also change and illuminate the light of Christ. However, obeying the Word cannot be accomplished only by one's own strength and willpower; the Holy Spirit must guide and help him.

When we hear and understand the Word, open our hearts, and accept Jesus as our Savior, God gives the Holy Spirit as a gift. The Holy Spirit resides in people who accept Jesus as their Savior, and helps them hear and understand the Word of truth. The Scripture tells us that *"Flesh gives birth to flesh, but the Spirit gives birth to spirit"* (John 3:6). The children of God who receive the Holy Spirit as a gift can rid themselves everyday of sin and evil by the power of the Holy Spirit, and become spiritual people.

Are any of you anxious and worried, thinking, 'How am I to keep all those commands?'

1 John 5:2-3 remind us, *"This is how we know that we love the children of God: by loving God and carrying out his commands. This is love for God: to obey his commands. And his commands are not burdensome."* If you love God from the depths of your heart, obeying His commands could not be difficult.

When parents give birth to their children, the parents look after every aspect of their child including feeding, clothing, bathing, and the like. On the one hand, if the parents are looking after a child not their own, it may feel burdensome. On the other hand, if the parents are looking after their own child, it can never feel burdensome. Even if the child wakes up and cries in the middle of the night, the parents do not feel bothered; they simply love their child too much. Doing something for a loved one is a source of great joy and happiness; it is not difficult or irritating. By the same token, if we truly believe that God is the Father of our spirits and, in His immeasurable love, gave His one and only Son to be crucified on a cross for us, how could we not love Him? Moreover, if we love God, living by His Word would not be arduous. Instead, it will be arduous and agonizing when we do not live by God's Word or obey His will.

I had suffered from a variety of diseases for seven years until my older sister led me to a sanctuary of God. Through receiving the fire of the Holy Spirit and the healing of all my diseases at the moment I knelt down in the sanctuary, I met the living God. This was April 17, 1974. Thenceforth, I started attending all types of worship services in full gratitude of God's grace. In November of that year, I attended my first revival meeting at which I began to learn His Word, the fundamentals of one's life in Christ:

'Ah, this is what God's like!'
'I must cast all my sins away.'
'This is what happens when I believe!'
'I must quit smoking and drinking.'
'I am to pray continually.'
'Giving tithes is mandatory,
and I am not to come before God empty-handed.'

All week long, I received the Word only with "Amen!" in my heart.

After that revival meeting, I quit smoking and drinking, and began giving tithes and thanksgiving offerings. I also began praying at dawn and gradually became a man of prayer. I did exactly as I had learned, and started to read the Bible as well.

I was healed of all my diseases and infirmities, none of which I could heal by any worldly means, by the power of God in an instant. Therefore, I could wholly believe in every verse and chapter of the Bible. Since I was a beginner in faith at the time, there were some parts of the Scripture I could not comprehend easily. Yet, the commands I could understand I began obeying immediately. For instance, when the Bible told me not to lie, in turn I told myself, "Lying is a sin! The Bible tells me I mustn't lie, so I will not lie." I also prayed, "God, please help me cast away inadvertent lying!" It was not that I had deceived people with an evil heart, but nevertheless I steadfastly prayed so that I could stop even inadvertent lying.

Many people lie, and most of them do not realize they lie. When someone, with whom you would not like to talk on the telephone, calls, have you ever nonchalantly asked your children, co-workers, or friends to "Tell him I'm not

The Author Rev. Dr. Jaerock Lee

here"? Many people lie because they are "considerate" of others. Such people lie when, for instance, they are asked if they would like anything to eat or drink upon visiting others. Even though they have not eaten or are thirsty, the guests who do not want to be "burdensome" often tell their hosts, "No, thank you. I had something to eat (or drink) before I came here." However, after I came to know that lying even with good intentions was still lying, I prayed continually to cast off lying and in the end I could even throw away inadvertent lies.

Moreover, I made a list of everything evil and sinful I was to cast off, and prayed. Only when I became convinced that I had surely cast off one evil and sinful habit or deed after another, did I cross that item out with a red pen. If there was anything evil and sinful I could not easily cast off even after determined prayer, I began fasting without delay. If I could not do it after a three-day fasting, I extended the fasting to five days. If I repeated the same sin, then I embarked on a seven-day fasting. However, rarely did I have to fast for a week; after a three-day fasting, I could cast off most of sins and evil. As much as I cast off evil through repeating such processes, I became even cleaner a vessel.

Three years after I met the Lord, I threw away everything disobedient to the Word of God and could be deemed a clean vessel in His sight. In addition, as I dutifully and diligently kept commands, including "Do's" and "Keep's," I could come to live by His Word in a short amount of time. As I transformed into a clean vessel, God blessed me abundantly. My family received the blessings of health. I could promptly pay off all the debts. I received blessings both physical and spiritual. This is because, the Bible assures us as follows: *"Dear friends, if our hearts do not condemn us, we have confidence before God and receive from him anything we ask, because we obey his commands and do what pleases him"* (1 John 3:21-22).

Second, in order to become a vessel more beautiful than a jewel, you must be "refined by fire" and illuminate the spiritual light.

Expensive gemstones on rings and necklaces had once been impure. However, they have been refined by lapidaries and come to give out brilliant lights and possess beautiful shapes.

Just as these skilled lapidaries cut, polish, and refine by fire these gemstones and turn them into gorgeous shapes with great luster, God disciplines His children. God disciplines them not because of their sins, but so that through the discipline He may physically and spiritually bless them. In the eyes of His children who have not sinned or committed any wrong, it may seem that they have to endure the pain and suffering of trials. This is a process through which God trains and disciplines His children so that they may illuminate more beautiful colors and luster. 1 Peter 2:19 reminds us that, *"For it is commendable if a man bears up under the pain of unjust suffering because he is conscious of God."* We also read that, *"These have come so that your faith – of greater worth than gold, which perishes even though refined by fire – may be proved genuine and may result in praise, glory and honor when Jesus Christ is revealed"* (1 Peter 1:7).

Even if the children of God have already cast off every kind of evil and become sanctified vessels, at the time of His choosing, God allows them to be disciplined and tried so that they will come forth as vessels more beautiful than jewels. As the latter half of 1 John 1:5 tells us, *"God is light; in him there is no darkness at all,"* because God is the glorious light itself without a flaw or a blemish, He leads His children to the same level of light.

Therefore, when you overcome any God-allowed trials in goodness and love, you will become a more gleaming and beautiful vessel. The level of spiritual authority and power is different according to the brightness of the spiritual light. In addition, when the spiritual light shines, the enemy devil and Satan have no place to stand.

In Mark 9 is a scene in which Jesus drove out an evil spirit from a boy whose father begged Jesus to heal his son. Jesus rebuked the evil spirit. "You deaf and mute spirit, I command you, come out of him and never enter him again." The evil spirit left the boy, who became sound again. Prior to this scene is another episode in which the father brought his son to Jesus' disciples, who could not drive the evil spirit out. That is because the disciples' level of spiritual light and Jesus' level of spiritual light were different.

What, then, must we do if we are to enter Jesus' level of spiritual light? We can be victorious in any trials by steadfastly believing in God, overcoming evil with good, and even loving the enemy. Consequently, once your goodness, love, and righteousness are deemed genuine, just like Jesus, you can drive out evil spirits and heal any diseases and infirmities.

Blessings for Vessels More Beautiful than Jewels

As I have walked the path of faith over the years, I

have also endured countless trials. For instance, at the accusation of a television program a few years ago, I endured a trial that was as painful and agonizing as death. As fallout, people who had received grace through me and many others whom I had long considered as close as family betrayed me.

To worldly people, I became a subject of misunderstanding and a target of blame, while many Manmin members suffered and were wrongfully persecuted. Nonetheless, Manmin members and I overcame that trial with goodness and, as we surrendered everything to God, we begged the God of love and mercy to forgive them.

Moreover, I did not hate or forsake those who had left and made things difficult for the church. In the midst of this excruciating trial, I faithfully believed that my Father God loved me. This is how I could face even those who had done evil only in goodness and love. As a student receives recognition for his hard work and merit through an examination, once my faith, goodness, love, and righteousness received God's recognition, He blessed me to perform and manifest His power all the more greatly.

After the trial, He opened the door through which I was to accomplish the world mission. God worked so that tens of thousands, hundreds of thousands, and even millions of people would gather at overseas crusades I conducted, and He has been with me with His power that transcends time and space.

The spiritual light with which God surrounds us is more luminous and beautiful than that of any jewels of this world. God considers those of His children whom He surrounds with the spiritual light to be vessels more beautiful than jewels.

Therefore, may each of you quickly accomplish sanctification and become a vessel that illuminates the trial-proven spiritual light and is more beautiful than a jewel, so that you will receive whatever you ask and lead a blessed life, in the name of our Lord Jesus Christ I pray!

Message 4

The Light

1 John 1:5

This is the message
we have heard from him
and declare to you:
God is light;
in him there is
no darkness at all.

There are many kinds of lights and in each of them is its own wondrous ability. Above all, it brightens darkness, provides warmth, and kills harmful bacteria or fungi. With light, plants can sustain life through photosynthesis.

However, there are the physical light we can see with our naked eyes and touch, and the spiritual light we cannot see or touch. Just as the physical light has many abilities, in the spiritual light are an immeasurable number of abilities. When light shines at nighttime, darkness fades away immediately. In the same way, when the spiritual light shines in our life, spiritual darkness will quickly fade away as we walk in God's love and mercy. Since spiritual darkness is the root of illnesses and problems at home, work, and in relationships, we cannot find true comfort. However, when the spiritual light shines on our lives, problems that are beyond the limit of man's knowledge and skills can be resolved and all our desires answered.

The Spiritual Light

What is the spiritual light and how does it work? We find in the latter half of 1 John 1:5 that *"God is light; in him there is no darkness at all,"* and in John 1:1, *"the Word was God."* In sum, "the light" refers not only to God Himself, but also His Word that is the truth, goodness, and love. Before the creation of all things, in the vastness of the universe God existed alone and not put on any shape. As a union of the light and the sound, God harbored the entire universe. The brilliant, magnificent, and beautiful light surrounded the whole universe and from that light came out an elegant, clear, and sonorous voice.

God who existed as the light and the sound designed the providence of the cultivation of mankind to reap true children. He then put on one shape, separated Himself into the Trinity, and in His own image created mankind. However, the essence of God is still the light and the sound, and He still works by the light and the sound. Even though He is in the shape of a human being, in that shape are the light and the sound of His infinite power.

In addition to God's power, there are other elements of the truth, including love and goodness in this spiritual light. The sixty-six books in the Bible are a collection of truths of the spiritual light that are uttered in a sound. In other words, "the light" refers to all the commands and verses in the Bible regarding goodness, righteousness, and love, including "Love one another," "Pray unceasingly," "Keep the Sabbath," "Obey the Ten Commandments," and the like.

Walk in the Light in Order to Meet God

While God governs the world of light, the enemy devil and Satan govern the world of darkness. Moreover, since the enemy devil and Satan oppose God, people living in the world of darkness cannot meet God. Therefore, in order to meet God, have a variety of your problems in life resolved, and receive answers, you must quickly come out of the world of darkness and enter the world of light.

In the Bible we find many *"Do"* commands. These include "Love one another," "Serve each other," "Pray," "Be thankful," and the like. There are also *"Keep"* commands, including "Keep the Sabbath," "Keep the Ten Commandments," "Keep God's commands," and the like. Then there are many *"Do not"* commands, including, "Do not lie," "Do not hate," "Do not seek your own good," "Do not worship idols," "Do not steal," "Do not be jealous," "Do not envy," "Do not gossip," and the like. There are also *"Cast away"* commands, including "Cast away all kinds of evil," "Throw away envy and jealousy," "Cast away greed," and the like.

On the one hand, obeying these commands of God is living in the light, resembling our Lord, and resembling our Father God. On the other hand, if you do not do as God tells you, if you do not keep what He tells you to keep, if you do what He tells you not to do, and if you do not throw away what He tells you to throw away, you will continue to remain in the darkness. Therefore, remembering that disobeying God's Word means we are in the world of darkness governed by the enemy devil and Satan, we must always live by His Word and walk in the light.

Fellowship with God When We Walk in the Light

As the first half of 1 John 1:7 tells us, *"But if we walk in the light, as he is in the light, we have fellowship with one another,"* only when we walk and dwell in the light can we be said to have fellowship with God.

Just as there is fellowship between a father and his children, we must also have fellowship with God, the Father of our spirits. However, in order to establish and maintain fellowship with Him, we have to meet one requirement: throw away sin by walking in the light. That is why, *"If we claim to have fellowship with [God] yet walk in the darkness, we lie and do not live by the truth"* (1 John 1:6).

"Fellowship" is not one-sided. Just because you know of someone, that does not mean you have fellowship with that person. Only when both sides become close enough to know, trust, depend on, and converse with each other can there be "fellowship" between the both parties.

For example, most of you know the king or president of your country. No matter how well you may know or know about the president, if he does not know you, there is no fellowship between you and the president. Moreover, in fellowship there are different depths to it. The two of you may merely be an acquaintance; the two of you may be a little closer enough to ask how each other is doing from time to time; or, the two of you may have an intimate relationship in which you share even the deepest secrets.

This is the same with the fellowship with God. In order for our relationship with Him to be true fellowship, God has to know and acknowledge us. If we have profound fellowship with God, we will not be ill or weak, and there will be nothing to which we would not receive answers. God wants to give His children only the best promised, as He tells us in Deuteronomy 28 that if we fully obey our

God and carefully follow all His commands, we will be blessed when we come in and blessed when we go out; we will lend but borrow from no one; and we will be the head and not the tail.

Fathers of Faith Who Had True Fellowship with God

What kind of fellowship did David, whom God deemed *"a man after my own heart"* (Acts 13:22), have with Him? David loved, feared, and depended completely on God at all times. When he was running from Saul or going out to battle, like a child asking one by one his parent what he should do, David always asked, "Shall I go? Where shall I go?" and did as God commanded him. Moreover, God always gave David gentle and detailed answers, and as David did as God told him he could achieve victory after victory (2 Samuel 5:19-25).

David could enjoy a beautiful relationship with God because, with his faith, David pleased God. For instance, early in King Saul's reign, the Philistines invaded Israel. The Philistines were led by Goliath, who mocked Israel's troops and blasphemed and defied the name of God. Yet, no one from the camp of Israel dared to challenge Goliath. At that time, even though he was still a young man, David went to face Goliath unarmed and only with five smooth stones from the stream because he believed in the omnipotent God of Israel and that the battle belonged to God (1 Samuel 17). God worked so that David's stone would strike Goliath's forehead. After Goliath died, the tide turned, and Israel achieved a total victory.

For his firm faith, David was deemed a man after God's own heart, and as if a father and a son with an intimate relationship would discuss every affair, David could achieve all things with God by his side.

The Bible also tells us that God spoke with Moses face to face. For instance, when Moses boldly asked God to show His face, God was eager to give him everything he asked (Exodus 33:18). How could Moses have a close and intimate relationship with God?

Soon after Moses led the Israelites out of Egypt, he fasted and communicated with God for forty days atop Mount Sinai. When Moses' return was being delayed, the Israelites created an idol they could worship. Upon seeing this, God told Moses that He would destroy the Israelites and then He would make Moses into a great nation (Exodus 32:10).

At this, Moses pleaded with God: *"Turn from your fierce anger; relent and do not bring disaster on your people"* (Exodus 32:12b). The next day, he begged God again: *"Oh, what a great sin these people have committed! They have made themselves gods of gold. But now, please forgive their sin – but if not, then blot me out of the book you have written"* (Exodus 32:31-32). What amazing and earnest prayers of love they are!

Furthermore, we find in Numbers 12:3, *"Now Moses was a very humble man, more humble than anyone else on the face of the earth."* Numbers 12:7 reads, *"But this is not true of my servant Moses; he is faithful in all my house."* With his great love and meek heart, Moses could be faithful in all His house and enjoy an intimate fellowship with God.

Blessings for People Who Walk in the Light

Jesus, who came to the world as the light of the world, taught only the truth and the gospel of heaven. People in the work of darkness who belonged to the enemy devil, however, could not understand the light even when it was explained. In their opposition, people in the world of darkness could not accept the light and receive salvation, but instead went to the path of destruction.

People of good hearts come to see their sins, repent of

them, and reach salvation through the light of truth. By following the desires of the Holy Spirit, they also give birth to spirit on a daily basis and walk in the light. The lack of wisdom or ability on their part is no longer a problem. They will establish communion with God who is light, and receive the voice and supervision of the Holy Spirit. Then everything will go well with them and they will receive wisdom from heaven. Even if they have problems that are tangled like a spider's web, nothing can deter them from solving the problems and no hurdles can block their path because the Holy Spirit will personally instruct them each step of the way.

As 1 Corinthians 3:18 urges us, *"Do not deceive yourselves. If any one of you thinks he is wise by the standards of this age, he should become a 'fool,'"* we must realize that wisdom of the world is foolish before God.

Moreover, as James 3:17 tells us, *"But the wisdom that comes from heaven is first of all pure; then peace-loving, considerate, submissive, full of mercy and good fruit, impartial and sincere."* When we accomplish sanctification and go into the light, wisdom from heaven will descend on us. When we walk in the light, we will also reach a level at which we are happy even if we lack, and we do not feel like we lack anything even if we do indeed lack.

The apostle Paul confesses in Philippians 4:11, *"I have learned to be content whatever the circumstances."* By the same token, if we walk in the light we will accomplish God's peace, by which peace and joy will spring out and overflow within us. People who make peace with others will not quarrel or be hostile towards their family. Instead, as love and grace overflow in their hearts, confessions of thanksgiving will not cease from their lips.

Furthermore, when we walk in the light and resemble God as much as we are able, as He tells us in 3 John 1:2, *"Dear friends, I pray that you may enjoy good health and that all may go well with you, even as your soul is getting along well,"* we will surely receive not only the blessings of prosperity in everything, but also the authority, ability, and power of God who is light.

After Paul met the Lord and walked in the light, God enabled him to manifest astounding power as an apostle to the Gentiles. Even though Stephen or Philip was not a prophet or one of Jesus' disciples, God still worked greatly through them. In Acts 6:8, we find that *"Now Stephen, a man full of God's grace and power, did great wonders and miraculous signs among the people."* In Acts 8:6-7, we also find, *"When the crowds heard Philip and saw the miraculous signs he did, they all paid close attention to what he said. With shrieks, evil spirits came out of many, and many paralytics and cripples were healed."*

One can manifest God's power to the extent he becomes sanctified by walking in the light and resembling the Lord. There have been only a few people who manifested God's power. Yet, even among those who could manifest His power, the magnitude of the power manifested differed from one to another according to how much each person resembled God who is light.

'Am I Living in the Light?'

In order to receive the amazing blessing bestowed upon those who walk in the light, each of us must first ask and examine ourselves, "Am I living in the light?"

Even if you do not have a specific problem(s), you ought to examine yourself to see if you have led a "lukewarm" life in Christ, or if you have not heard and not been governed by the Holy Spirit. If so, you must wake up from your spiritual slumber.

If you have cast off some degree and amount of evil,

you should not be satisfied; as a child matures into an adult, you must also reach the faith of fathers. You ought to have communion of great depths with God as well as an intimate fellowship with Him.

If you are running towards sanctification, you must detect even the minutest remnants of evil and root them out. The more authority you have and the more of a head you become, you must always first serve and seek the interests of others. When others, including those who are less than you, point out your wrongs, you must be able to heed it. Instead of feeling resentment or discomfort and alienating those who go astray from the ways of man and do evil, in love and kindness you must be able to tolerate and move them poignantly. You must not discount or hold anyone contempt. Neither should you disregard others in your own righteousness nor destroy peace.

I have shown and given more love to the younger, the poorer, and the weaker of people. Like parents who care more for their weak and ill children than the healthy ones, I prayed harder for people in such situations, never disregarded them once, and tried to serve them from the center of my heart. Those who walk in the light must have compassion for even people who have done great wrong, and be able to forgive them and cover their faults instead of exposing their guilt.

Even in doing God's work, you must not put up or expose your own merit or accomplishment, but acknowledge the effort of others with whom you have worked. When their efforts are acknowledged and commended, you ought to be happier and more joyous.

Can you imagine how much God would love those of His children whose hearts resemble the heart of our Lord? The way He walked with Enoch for 300 years, God will walk with His children who resemble Him. Moreover, He will give them not only the blessings of health and everything's going well in all affairs, but also His power by which He will use them as precious vessels.

Therefore, even if you think that you have faith and love God, may you reexamine how much of your faith and love He will actually acknowledge, and walk in the light so that your life can overflow with evidences of His love and fellowship with Him, in the name of our Lord Jesus Christ I pray!

Message 5

The Power of the Light

1 John 1:5

This is the message
we have heard from him
and declare to you:
God is light;
in him there is
no darkness at all.

In the Bible, there are many instances in which countless people received salvation, healings, and answers through the truly astonishing work of God's power manifested by His Son Jesus. When Jesus commanded, all kinds of diseases were immediately healed and the infirmities were strengthened and restored.

The blind could see, the mute came to speak, and the deaf began to hear. A man with a shriveled hand was cured, the lame began walking again, and the paralytics received healing. Moreover, evil spirits were driven out and the dead revived.

These astonishing works of God's power were manifested not only by Jesus, but also by many prophets of Old Testament times and apostles of New Testament times. Of course, Jesus' manifestation of God's power could not equal that of prophets and apostles. Nonetheless, to people who resembled Jesus and God Himself, He gave them power and used them as His vessels. God who is light manifested His power through deacons like Stephen and Philip because they accomplished sanctification by walking in the light and resembling the Lord.

The Apostle Paul was Even Considered "God"

Among all the characters from the New Testament, the apostle Paul's manifestation of God's power ranked second after that of Jesus. He preached the gospel to the Gentiles, who did not know God, the messages of authority which were accompanied by signs and wonders. With this kind of power, Paul could testify to God the true Deity and Jesus Christ.

From the fact that idol worshiping and incantation were rampant at the time, there must have been some people among the Gentiles who deluded others. Spreading the gospel to such people required manifestation of the work of God's power that far surpassed the power of false incantation and the work of evil spirits (Romans 15:18-19).

From Acts 14:8 onward is a scene in which the apostle Paul preached the gospel in a region called Lystra. When Paul commanded a man who had been lame all his life, "Stand up on your feet!" the man stood up and started to walk (Acts 14:10). When people saw this, they confessed, "The gods have come down to us in human form" (Acts 14:11).

In Acts 28 is a scene in which Paul arrived on the island of Malta after a shipwreck. When he gathered a pile of brushwood and put it on the fire, a viper, driven out by the heat, fastened itself on his hand. Upon seeing this, the islanders expected him to swell up or suddenly fall dead, but when nothing happened to Paul, the people said he was a god (v. 6).

For the apostle Paul possessed a heart that was proper in the sight of God, he could manifest the work of His power even so that he was deemed a "god" by people.

The Power of God Who is Light

The power is given not because someone desires it; it is given only to those who resemble God and have accomplished sanctification. Even today, God is seeking people to whom He can give His power to use as vessels of glory. That is why Mark 16:20 reminds us that, *"then the disciples went out and preached everywhere, and the Lord worked with them and confirmed his word by the signs that accompanied it."* We also find in John 4:48, *"'Unless you people see miraculous signs and wonders,' Jesus told him, 'you will never believe.'"*

Leading countless people to salvation calls for the power from heaven that can manifest signs and wonders, which in turn testifies to the living God. In an age in which sin and evil especially thrive, signs and wonders are all the more required.

When we walk in the light and become one in spirit with our Father God, we can manifest the magnitude of power which Jesus manifested. This is because our Lord has promised, *"I tell you the truth, anyone who has faith in me will do what I have been doing. He will do even greater things than these, because I am going to the Father"* (John 14:12).

If anyone manifests the kind of power of the spiritual realm that is possible only by God, then he is to be recognized as of God. As Psalm 62:11 reminds us, *"God hath spoken once; twice have I heard this; that power belongeth unto God" (King James Version),* the enemy devil and Satan cannot manifest the kind of power that belongs to God. Of course, because they are spiritual beings they possess superior power to delude people and compel them to oppose God. One factor, however, remains certain: no other being can imitate the power of God, by which He controls life, death, blessing, curse, and history of mankind, and creates something from nothing. The power belongs to the realm of God who is light, and can be manifested only by those who have accomplished sanctification and reached the measure of faith of Jesus Christ.

Differences among God's Authority, Ability, and Power

In designating or referring to the ability of God, many people equate authority to ability, or ability to power; however, there is a pellucid difference among the three.

"Ability" is the power of faith by which something impossible to man is possible to God. "Authority" is the solemn, dignified, and majestic power God has established, and in the spiritual realm the state of sinlessness is power. In other words, authority is sanctification itself, and those sanctified children of God who have thoroughly cast off evil and untruth in their hearts can receive the spiritual authority.

What, then, is "power"? It refers to the ability and authority of God which He bestows upon those who have avoided every kind of evil and become sanctified.

Take this for an example. If a driver has the "ability" to drive a vehicle, then the traffic officer who directs the traffic has the "authority" to pull over any vehicles. This authority – to pull over and send any vehicles back on the road – has been given to the officer by the government. Therefore, even though the driver has the "ability" to drive a vehicle, since he lacks the "authority" of a traffic officer, when the officer tells the driver to either stop or go, the driver must heed.

In this way, authority and ability differ from one another, and when authority and ability are combined, we call it power. In Matthew 10:1, Jesus *"called his twelve disciples to him and gave them authority to drive out evil spirits and to heal every disease and sickness."* Power entails both the "authority" to drive out evil spirits and the "ability" to heal all diseases and infirmities.

Difference between the Gift of Healing and Power

Those who are unfamiliar with the power of God who is light often equate it to the gift of healing. The gift of healing in 1 Corinthians 12:9 refers to the work of scorching virus-infected diseases. It cannot cure deafness and muteness resulting from the degeneration of body parts or the death of nerve cells. Such cases of diseases and infirmities can be healed only by the power of God and by prayer of faith that pleases Him. Moreover, while the power of God who is light is manifested at all times, the gift of healing does not always work.

On the one hand, God gives the gift of healing to those, regardless of the extent of people's sanctification of the heart, who love and pray a great deal for others and their spirits, and whom God considers to be bold and useful vessels. However, if the gift of healing were used not for His glory but in an improper way and for one's own benefits, God will certainly take it back.

On the other hand, the power of God is given only to those who have accomplished sanctification of the heart; once given, it does not weaken or wither because the recipient will never use it for his own benefits. Instead, the more one resembles the heart of the Lord, the higher levels of power God will bestow upon him. If the heart and behavior of an individual become one with the Lord, he can manifest even the very work of God's power Jesus Himself manifested.

There are differences in the ways in which God's power are manifested. The gift of healing cannot cure grave or rare illnesses and it is more difficult for those with little faith to be cured by the gift of healing. However, by the power of God who is light, nothing is impossible. When the patient displays even a small proof of his faith, healing by God's power takes place immediately. Here, "faith" refers to spiritual faith by which one believes from the center of his heart.

Four Levels of the Power of God Who is Light

Through Jesus Christ who is the same yesterday and today, anyone who is deemed a suitable vessel in God's sight will manifest His power.

There are many different levels in manifestation of God's power. The more you accomplish spirit, the higher level of power you will enter and receive. People whose spiritual eyes are opened can see different levels of illumination of lights according to each level of the power of God. Human beings as creatures can manifest up to the four levels of God's power.

The first level of power is the manifestation of God's power by the red light, which destroys by the fire of the Holy Spirit.

The fire of the Holy Spirit spurted from the first level of power that is manifested by the red light burns and heals diseases including germ- and virus-infected diseases. Illnesses including cancer, lung disease, diabetes, leukemia, kidney disease, arthritis, heart trouble, and AIDS can be healed. This does not mean, however, that all of the diseases above can be healed at the first level of power. Those who already stepped beyond the

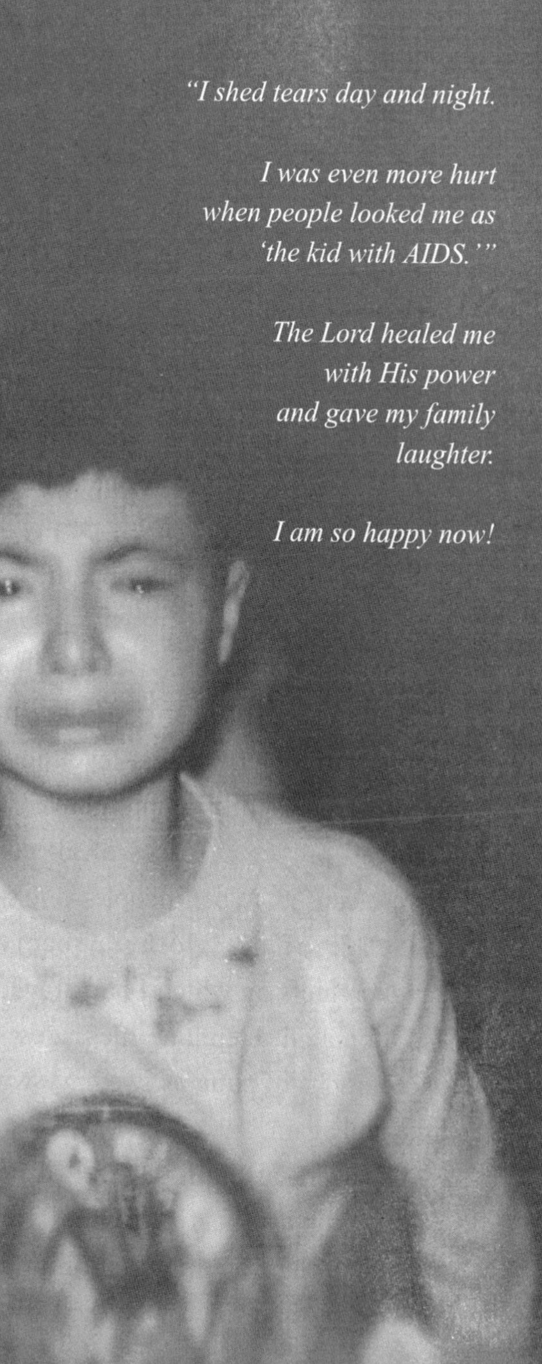

"I shed tears day and night.
I was even more hurt
when people looked me as
'the kid with AIDS.'"
The Lord healed me
with His power
and gave my family
laughter.
I am so happy now!

Esteban Juninka of Honduras, healed of AIDS

boundary of life God has set, such as in the case of the last stage of cancer or lung disease, the first level of power will not suffice.

Restoration of body parts that have been damaged or are unable to properly function requires greater power that will not only heal but also rebuild new body parts. Even in such a case, the degree of the patient's display of his faith as well as the degree of his family's display of their faith in love for him will determine the level at which God will manifest His power.

Since the founding, there have been countless manifestations of the first-level power at Manmin Joong-ang Church. When people obeyed the Word of God and received prayer, diseases of all conditions and severity were cleansed. When people shook my hands or touched the edge of my clothes, received prayer through handkerchiefs on which I had prayed, and prayer recorded as automated telephone messages, or when I prayed on photographs of patients, we have witnessed God's healing time and again.

The work at the first level of power is not limited to destroying by the fire of the Holy Spirit. Even for a moment, when one prays in faith and becomes inspired, affected by, and filled with the Holy Spirit, any individual can manifest even greater work of God's power. Yet, this is a temporary occurrence and not an evidence of permanently embedded power of God, occurring only when it is suitable to His will.

The second level of power is the manifestation of God's power by the blue light.

Malachi 4:2 tells us, *"But for you who revere my name, the sun of righteousness will rise with healing in its wings. And you will go out and leap like calves released from the stall."* People whose spiritual eyes are opened can see rays of laser-like lights emanating beams of healing.

The second level of power drives away darkness and frees people who are demon-possessed, Satan-controlled, and dominated by various types of evil spirits. A range of mental illnesses brought on by the force of darkness, including autism, nervous breakdown, and others are healed by the second-level power.

These kinds of diseases can be prevented if we are "joyful always" and "give thanks in all circumstances." Instead of being joyful always and giving thanks in all circumstances, if you come to hate others, harbor ill feelings, think negatively, and become easily angered, then you will be more vulnerable to such diseases. When the forces of Satan, which drive man to possess an evil thought and heart, are driven away, all those mental diseases will be naturally healed.

From time to time, by the second level of God's power, physical diseases and infirmities are healed. Such diseases and infirmities wrought by the work of demons and devils are healed by the light of the second level of God's power. Here, "infirmities" refer to the degeneration and paralysis of body parts, as in the case of those who are mute, deaf, crippled, blind, paralyzed from birth, and the like.

From Mark 9:14 onward is a scene in which Jesus drove out a "deaf and mute spirit" from a boy (v. 25). This boy had become deaf and mute because of an evil spirit within him. When Jesus drove out the spirit, the boy was immediately healed.

By the same token, when the cause of a disease is the force of darkness, including demons, the evil spirits must be driven out in order for the patient to be healed. If one suffers from problems in his digestive system as fallout of nervous breakdown, the cause must be rooted out by driving out the force of Satan. In such diseases as paralysis and arthritis, the work of the force and remnants of darkness can also be found. Sometimes, although medical diagnosis cannot detect anything physically wrong, people suffer from pain here and there in their

"I saw the light...

I finally got out of
the fourteen-year-long tunnel...

I had given up on myself,
but I was reborn
by the power of the Lord!"

Shama Masaz of Pakistan, released from 14-year demon-possession

bodies. When I pray for anyone suffering in this manner, others whose spiritual eyes are opened often see the force of darkness in abominable animal shapes leaving the patient's body.

In addition to the forces of darkness found in diseases and infirmities, the second level of power of God, who is light, can also drive out the forces of darkness found at home, business, and work. When an individual who can manifest the second level of God's power visits those suffering from persecution at home and troubles at work and business, as darkness is driven out and the light comes upon people, blessings according to their deeds descend upon them.

Raising the dead or terminating someone's life according to the will of God is the work of the second level of God's power as well. The following instances fall into this category: the apostle Paul's raising of Eutychus (Acts 20:9-12); Ananias and Sapphira's deception of the apostle Peter and his consequent curse that resulted in their death (Acts 5:1-11); and Elisha's cursing of children that also resulted in their death (2 Kings 2:23-24).

There are, however, fundamental differences in the work of Jesus and those of the apostles Paul and Peter and Prophet Elisha. Ultimately, God as the Lord of all spirits had to allow whether for someone to live or be taken

"Oh, God!
How is this possible?
How is it possible that I walk?"

She came to walk
only after prayer from the pulpit (Kenya)

away. Yet, since Jesus and God are one and the same, what Jesus willed was what God willed. This is why Jesus could bring back the dead only by commanding them by His Word (John 11:43-44), while other prophets and apostles had to ask for the will of God and His approval to revive anyone.

The third level of power is the manifestation of God's power by the white or colorless light, and is accompanied by all types of signs and the work of creation.

At the third level of power of God who is light, all types of signs as well as the work of creation are manifested. Here, "signs" refer to healings through which the blind come to see, the mute speak, and the deaf hear. The crippled get up and walk, shortened legs are extended, and infantile paralysis or cerebral palsy is wholly healed. Deformed or completely degenerated body parts from birth are restored. Shattered bones are put back together, missing bones are created, short tongues grow, and tendons are reconnected. Moreover, since the lights of the first, second, and third levels of God's power are manifested simultaneously at the third level as necessary, no disease and infirmity will pose a problem.

*"Even I didn't want to
look at my body
that was thoroughly cooked...*

When I was alone,

*He came to me,
reached out His hand,
and put me by His side...*

*by His love and dedication
I have received a new life...*

*Is there anything
I couldn't do for the Lord?"*

Senior Deaconess Eundeuk Kim,
healed of the third-degree burn
from head to toe

Even if someone is burned from head to toe and his cells and muscles are burned, or even if the flesh is cooked by boiling water, God can create everything anew. As God can create something from nothing, He can fix not only inanimate objects such as machinery, but also human body parts that are not well.

At Manmin Joong-ang Church, through handkerchief prayer or prayer recorded as automated telephone messages, internal organs that have not functioned properly or been severely damaged are restored. As brutally damaged lungs are healed while kidneys and livers that need transplants become normal, at the third level of God's power, the work of the power of creation are unceasingly manifested.

There is one factor to be clearly differentiated. On the one hand, if the function of a body part that has been feeble is restored, that is the work of the first level of God's power. On the other hand, if the function of a body part which has had no chance of recovery is revived or created anew, that is the work of the third level of God's power, the power of the creation.

The fourth level of power is the manifestation of God's power by the gold light, and is the fruition of power.

As we can tell by the work of power manifested by Jesus, the fourth level of power governs all things, rules over the weather, and even orders inanimate objects to obey. In Matthew 21:19, when Jesus cursed a fig tree, we find that, "Immediately the tree withered." From Matthew 8:23 on is a scene in which Jesus rebuked the winds and the waves, and it was completely calm. Even the nature and such inanimate objects as the winds and the sea became obedient as Jesus commanded them.

Jesus once told Peter, "Put out into deep water, and let down the nets for a catch," and when Peter obeyed, he caught such a large number of fish that his nets began to break (Luke 5:4-6). At another time, Jesus told Peter, "Take the first fish you catch; open its mouth and you will find a four-drachma coin. Take it and give it to them for my tax and yours" (Matthew 17:24-27).

As God created all things in the universe by His Word, when Jesus commanded the universe, it obeyed Him and became real. By the same token, once we possess true faith, we will be sure of what we hope for and certain of what we do not see (Hebrews 11:1), and the work of power that creates all things from nothing will be manifested.

Furthermore, at the fourth level of God's power, the work is manifested transcending time and space.

Among Jesus' manifestations of God's power, a few of them transcended time and space. From Mark 7:24 on is a scene in which a woman begged Jesus to heal her demon-possessed daughter. Upon seeing the woman's humility and faith, Jesus told her, "You may go; the demon has left your daughter" (v. 29). When the woman returned home, she found her child lying on the bed, and the demon gone.

Even though Jesus did not visit each of the sick personally, when He saw the faith of the sick and commanded, healings that transcended time and space took place.

Jesus' walking on the water, which is the work of power He alone manifested, also testifies to the fact everything in the universe is under Jesus' authority.

Furthermore, Jesus tells us in John 14:12, *"I tell you the truth, anyone who has faith in me will do what I have been doing. He will do even greater things than these, because I am going to the Father."* As He assured us, truly astonishing work of God's power are manifested at Manmin Joong-ang Church today.

For instance, various wonders in which the weather is altered take place. When I pray, a pouring rain stops in the

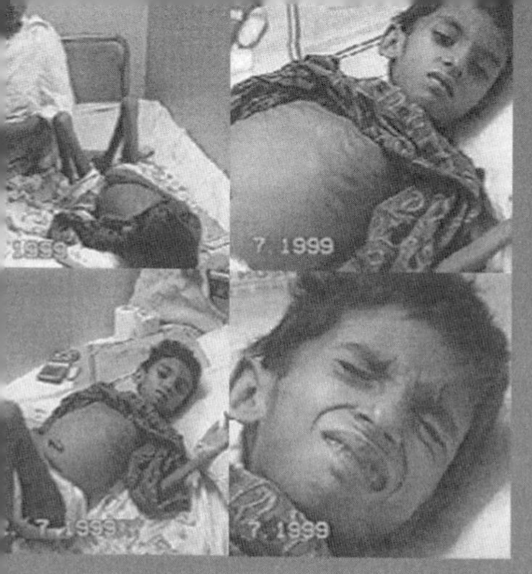

It's so painful

It's so painful
that I can't open my eyes...

No one knew what I felt,
but the Lord knew it all
and healed me."

Cynthia of Pakistan,
healed of Celiac disease and ileus

blink of an eye; a very dark cloud recedes; and a spotless sky is filled with clouds in an instant. There have also been countless instances in which inanimate objects obeyed my prayer. Even in the case of life-threatening carbon monoxide poisoning, a minute or two after my command, the person who had been unconscious came to recover and suffered from no side effects. When I prayed for an individual suffering from a third-degree burn, "Burning sensation, go away," the person no longer felt anything painful.

In addition, the work of God's power that transcends time and space is taking place all the more greatly and overwhelmingly. The case of Cynthia, daughter of Rev. Wilson John Gil, senior pastor of the Pakistan Manmin Church is particularly notable. When I prayed for Cynthia on her photograph in Seoul, Korea, a girl on whom the doctors had given up all hopes, quickly recovered from the moment I prayed for her from thousands of miles away.

At the fourth level of power, the power to heal diseases, drive away the forces of darkness, display signs and wonders, and command all things to obey – the combined work of the first, second, third, and fourth levels of power – are manifested.

The Most High Power of Creation

The Bible records Jesus' manifestations of power that are above the fourth level of power. This level of power, the Most High Power, belongs to the Creator. This power is manifested not at the same level at which human beings can manifest His power. Instead, it comes from the original light that illuminated when God existed alone.

In John 11, Jesus commanded Lazarus, who had been dead for four days and whose body reeked of a terrible odor, "Lazarus, come out!" At His command, the dead man came out, his hands and feet wrapped with strips of linen, and a cloth around his face (v. 43-44).

After a person has removed every kind of evil, become sanctified, come to resemble the heart of his Father God, and changed into a whole spirit, he will enter the spiritual realm. The more he gathers the knowledge of the spiritual realm, the higher his manifestation of God's power will rise above the fourth level.

At that time, he reaches the level of power, power that can only be manifested by the Deity, which is the Most High Power of Creation. When man wholly accomplishes this, as the time when God created everything in the universe by His command, he will also manifest wondrous work of creation.

For instance, when he commands a blind person, "Open your eyes," the blind man's eyes will be immediately opened. When he commands a mute person, "Speak!" the mute person will come to speak in an instant. When he commands a cripple, "Stand up," the crippled man will walk and run. When he commands, scars and body parts that have been decaying will be renewed.

This is accomplished by the light and the voice of God who had alone existed as light and voice since before the beginning of time. When the limitless power of creation in the light is drawn forth by the voice, the light descends and the work is manifested. This is the way for people, who have stepped beyond the boundary of life God has set, and diseases and infirmities that cannot be cured by the first, second, or third level of power, to be healed.

Receiving the Power of God who is light

How can we resemble the heart of God who is light, receive His power, and lead countless people to the way of salvation?

First, we must not only avoid every kind of evil

and accomplish sanctification, but also achieve the good of the heart and long for the uppermost good.

If you showed no signs of ill feelings or discomfort against an individual who made your life extremely difficult or harmed you, could you be said to have accomplished the good of the heart? No, that is not the case. Even if there is no shuddering of the heart or a sense of discomfort and you wait and endure, in the sight of God this is only the first step of the good.

At the higher level of the good, one will speak and behave in ways to move the people who make his life difficult or harm him. At the uppermost good with which God is pleased, one must be able to give up his own life for the sake of his enemy.

Jesus could forgive the people who were crucifying Him and for those people freely gave up His life because He possessed the uppermost good. Both Moses and the apostle Paul were willing to give their lives for the very people who were trying to kill them as well.

When God was about to destroy the people of Israel, who opposed with idol-worshiping, complained, and held a grudge against Him even as they witnessed great signs and wonders, how did Moses respond? He earnestly pleaded with God: *"But now, please forgive their sin – but if not, then blot me out of the book you have written"* (Exodus 32:32). The apostle Paul was the same. As he confessed in Romans 9:3, *"For I could wish that I myself were cursed and cut off from Christ for the sake of my brothers, those of my own race,"* Paul had accomplished the uppermost good and thus great work of God's power always accompanied him.

Next, we must accomplish spiritual love.

Love has abated considerably today. Although many people tell one another, "I love you," with the passing of time, we see that most of this "love" is fleshly love that changes. The love of God is spiritual love that sublimes day after day, and is described in detail in 1 Corinthians 13.

First, *"Love is patient [and] love is kind. It does not envy."* Our Lord has forgiven all our sins and flaws, and opened the way of salvation by patiently waiting even for those who are not forgivable. Yet, even though we confess our love for the Lord, are we quick to expose the sins and flaws of our brothers and sisters? Are we quick to judge and condemn others when something or someone is not to our liking? Have we been jealous of someone whose life is going well or felt disappointed?

Next, love *"does not boast [and] it is not proud."* Even if we may appear to be glorifying the Lord on the outside, if we have a heart wanting to be recognized by others, expose ourselves, and disregard or teach others because of our position or authority, it would be boasting and being proud.

Moreover, love *"is not rude, it is not self-seeking, it is not easily angered, [and] it keeps no record of wrongs."* Our rude behavior towards God and people, our fickle hearts and minds that easily change, our effort to be greater even at the expense of others, our easily-conceived ill feelings, our tendency to think negatively and evil of others, and the like, do not constitute love.

In addition, love *"does not delight in evil but rejoices in the truth."* If we have love, we must always walk and rejoice in the truth. As 3 John 1:4 tells us, *"I have no greater joy than to hear that my children are walking in the truth,"* the truth must be the source of our delight and happiness.

Lastly, love *"always protects, always trusts, always hopes, [and] always perseveres."* Those who truly love God come to know the will of God, and thus they come to believe all things. As people look forward to and earnestly believe in the return of our Lord, the resurrection of believers, heavenly awards, and the like, they hope for things above, endure all difficulties, and strive to accomplish His will.

In order to show evidences of His love for those who obey the truth such as the good, love, and others as recorded in the Bible, God who is light gives them His power as a gift. He is also eager to meet and answer all those who strive to walk in the light.

Therefore, by discovering yourself and rending your heart, may you who desire to receive God's blessings and answers become prepared vessels before Him and experience the power of God, in the name of our Lord Jesus Christ I pray!

Message 6

The Eyes of the Blind Will Open

John 9:32-33

Nobody has
ever heard of opening
the eyes of a man born blind.
If this man were not from God,
he could do nothing.

In Acts 2 is a scene in which Jesus' disciple Peter, after he received the Holy Spirit, spoke to the Jews by citing the words of Prophet Joel. *"Men of Israel,"* Peter told the crowd, *"listen to this: Jesus of Nazareth was a man accredited by God to you by miracles, wonders and signs, which God did among you through him, as you yourselves know."* Jesus' great manifestations of power, signs, and wonders were the evidences testifying that the Jesus the Jews crucified was indeed the Messiah whose coming had been foretold in the Old Testament.

Furthermore, Peter himself came to manifest God's power after having received and been empowered by the Holy Spirit. He healed a crippled beggar (Acts 3:8), and people even brought the sick into the streets and laid them on beds and mats so that at least Peter's shadow might fall on some of them as he passed by (Acts 5:15).

Since power is a voucher that testifies to God's presence with the one who manifests power and the surest way to plant a seed of faith in the hearts of unbelievers, God has given power to those He deemed fit.

Jesus Heals a Man Born Blind

The story of John 9 begins as Jesus came across a man born blind along His way. Jesus' disciples wanted to know why the blind man could not see from birth. "Rabbi, who sinned, this man or his parents, that he was born blind?" In reply, Jesus explained to them that the man was born blind so that the work of God might be displayed in his life. Then He spit on the ground, made some mud with the saliva, put it on the man's eyes, and commanded the man born blind, "Go wash in the Pool of Siloam." When the man obeyed immediately and washed in the Pool of Siloam, his eyes opened.

Even though there are many other people whom Jesus healed in the Bible, one difference sets this man born blind apart from all the rest. The man did not beg Jesus to heal him; instead, Jesus came to the man and completely healed him.

Why, then, did this man born blind receive such abundant grace?

First, the man was obedient.

To an ordinary person, none of what Jesus did – His spitting on the ground, making the mud, putting the mud on the blind man's eyes, and telling the man to go and wash in the Pool of Siloam – makes any sense. Common sense does not allow such an individual to believe that the eyes of a person born blind can be opened after putting some mud on his eyes and washing them in the water. Furthermore, if this person heard this command without knowing who Jesus was, he and the most of the people would not only disbelieve, but also become evidently angered. Yet, that was not the case with this man. As Jesus commanded, the man obeyed and washed his eyes in the Pool of Siloam. Ultimately and astonishingly, his eyes that had been shut since the moment he was born, were now opened for the first time and the man began to see.

If you think that the Word of God does not agree with man's common sense or experience, try to obey His Word with a humble heart like that of this man born blind. Then the grace of God will come upon you and, as the blind man's eyes were opened, you will also have wondrous experiences.

Second, the innately blind man's spiritual eyes, which could distinguish truth from untruth, were opened.

From his conversation with the Jews after he was

healed, we can tell that while the blind man's eyes were physically shut, in goodness of the heart he could tell apart right from wrong. On the contrary, the Jews were the spiritually blind, enclosed in the rigid boundary of the law. When the Jews asked for details of the healing, the man who had been blind boldly proclaimed, *"The man they call Jesus made some mud and put it on my eyes. He told me to go to Siloam and wash. So I went and washed, and then I could see"* (v. 11).

In disbelief, when the Jews cross-examined the man who had been blind, "What have you to say about him? It was your eyes he opened," the man responded, "He is a prophet" (v. 17). The man thought that if Jesus were powerful enough to heal blindness, He must have been a man of God. Ironically, the Jews rebuked the man: "Give glory to God. We know this man is a sinner" (v. 24).

How illogical is their claim? God does not answer the prayer of a sinner. Neither does He give power to a sinner to open a blind man's eyes and to receive glory. Even though the Jews could neither believe nor understand this, the man who had been blind continued to make bold and truthful confessions: *"We know that God does not listen to sinners. He listens to the godly man who does his will. Nobody has ever heard of opening the eyes of a man born blind. If this man were not from God, he could do nothing"* (v. 31-33).

As no blind eyes had ever been opened from the time of the creation, whoever heard the news of this man should have rejoiced and celebrated with him. Instead, amongst the Jews developed an air of judgment, condemnation, and hostility. Since the Jews were too spiritually ignorant, they thought that the work of God itself was the very act of opposing Him. The Bible tells us, however, that only God can open the eyes of the blind.

Psalm 146:8 reminds us that *"the LORD gives sight to the blind,"* while Isaiah 29:18 tells us, *"In that day the deaf will hear the words of the scroll, and out of gloom and darkness the eyes of the blind will see."* Isaiah 35:5 also tells us, *"Then will the eyes of the blind be opened and the ears of the deaf unstopped."* Here, "In that day" and "Then" refers to the time when Jesus came and opened the eyes of the blind.

Despite these passages and reminders, in their rigid boundary and evilness, the Jews could not believe the work of God manifested through Jesus, and instead charged that Jesus was a sinner who disobeyed the Word of God. Even though the man who had been blind did not possess a great deal of knowledge on the law, in his good conscience he knew the truth: that God does not listen to sinners. The man also knew that the healing of blind eyes was possible only by God.

Third, after receiving God's grace, the man who had been blind came before the Lord and resolved to lead a wholly new life.

To this day, I have witnessed countless instances in which people at the threshold of death received strength and answers to all kinds of problems in life at Manmin Joong-ang Church. I lament, however, for people whose hearts change even after they receive God's grace and others who forsake their faith and return to the ways of the world. When their lives are in pain and agony, such people come to pray in tears, "I will live only for the Lord once I'm healed." When they do receive healing and blessings, in the pursuit of their own benefits these people forsake grace and go astray from the truth. Even if they may have their physical problems solved, it is useless because their spirits have parted from the way of salvation and are on their way to hell.

This man who had been born blind had a good heart that would not forsake grace. That is why when he met Jesus, he was not only healed of blindness but also assured of the blessing of salvation. When Jesus asked him, "Do you believe in the Son of Man?" the man

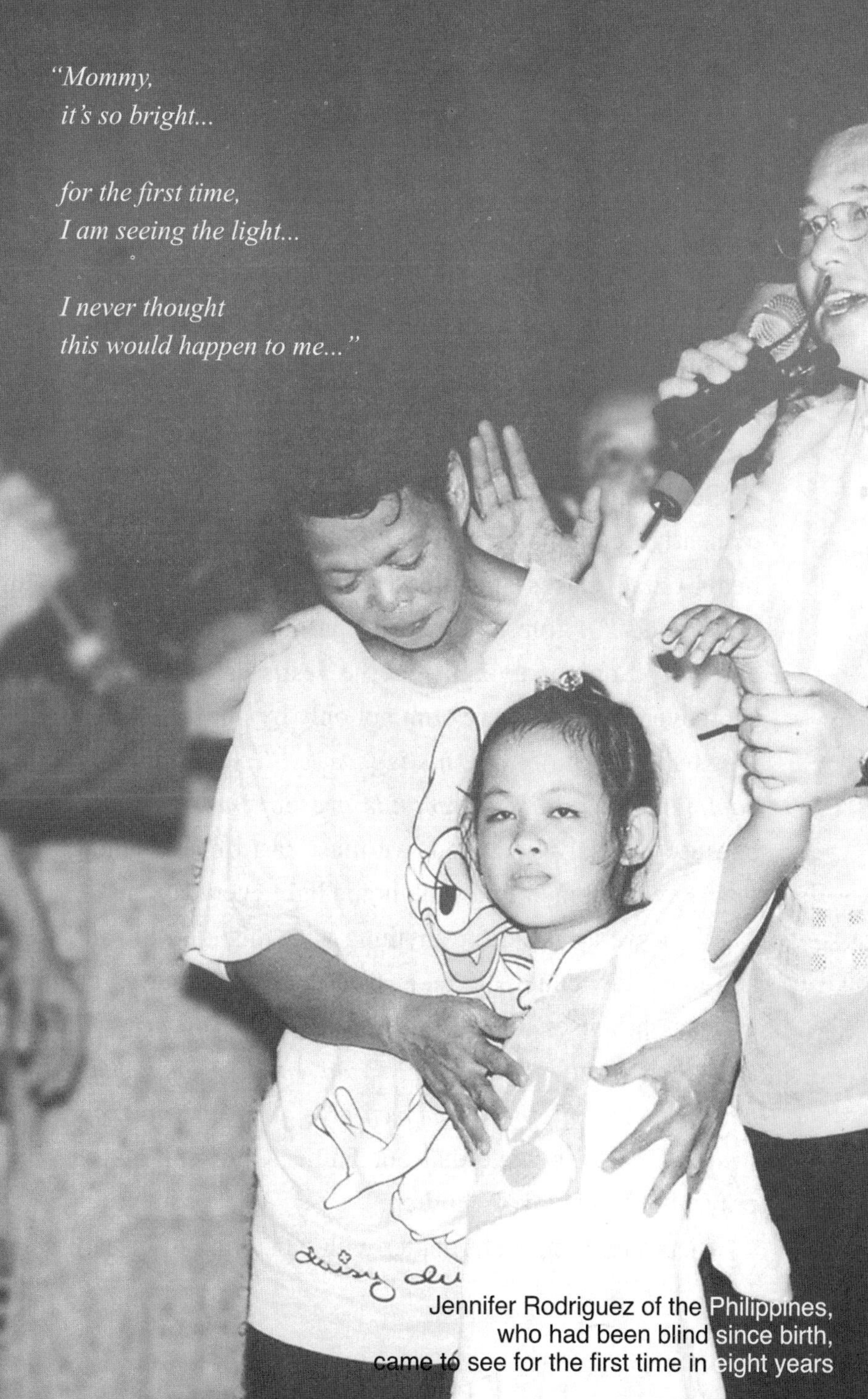

"Mommy,
it's so bright...

for the first time,
I am seeing the light...

I never thought
this would happen to me..."

Jennifer Rodriguez of the Philippines, who had been blind since birth, came to see for the first time in eight years

responded, "Who is he, sir? Tell me so that I may believe in him" (v. 35-36). When Jesus answered, "You have now seen him; in fact he is the one speaking with you," the man confessed, "Lord, I believe" (v. 37-38). The man did not simply "believe"; he was receiving Jesus as the Christ. It was the man's firm confession in which he resolved to follow only the Lord and live only for the Lord.

God wants all of us to come before Him with this kind of heart. He wants us to seek Him not just because He heals our diseases and blesses us. He longs for us to understand His true love that unsparingly gave His one and only Son for us and receive Jesus as our Savior. Moreover, we are to love Him not only by our lips. As He tells us in 1 John 5:3, *"This is love for God: to obey his commands. And his commands are not burdensome,"* because we truly love God, we must cast off everything that is evil within us and walk in the light everyday.

When we ask God for anything with this kind of faith and love, how could He not answer us? In Matthew 7:11, as Jesus promises us, *"If you, then, though you are evil, know how to give good gifts to your children, how much more will your Father in heaven give good gifts to those who ask him!"* believe that our Father God will answer prayers of His beloved children.

Therefore, it does not matter with what kind of disease

or problem you have come before God. With the confession, "Lord, I believe!" stemming from the center of your heart, when you display deeds of your faith, the Lord who healed a man born blind will heal any sorts of diseases, turn the impossible into the possible, and solve all your problems in life.

The Work of Opening the Eyes of the Blind at Manmin Joong-ang Church

Since the founding in 1982, Manmin has greatly glorified God through the work of opening the eyes of countless individuals who had been blind. Many people who had been blind since birth received sight after prayer. The sight of many others whose eyesight had deteriorated and relied on eyeglasses or contact lenses was restored. Among many, many astonishing testimonies, the following are a few examples.

When I conducted a Great United Crusade in Honduras in July 2002, there was a twelve-year-old girl named Maria who had lost the sight in her right eye after a severe fever at the age of two. Her parents made a variety of attempts in vain to restore her sight. Even the cornea transplant Maria received was of no use. During the

"My heart led me
to that place...

I only longed for grace...

God gave me a huge present.

What makes me happier
than seeing is the fact
that I met the living God!"

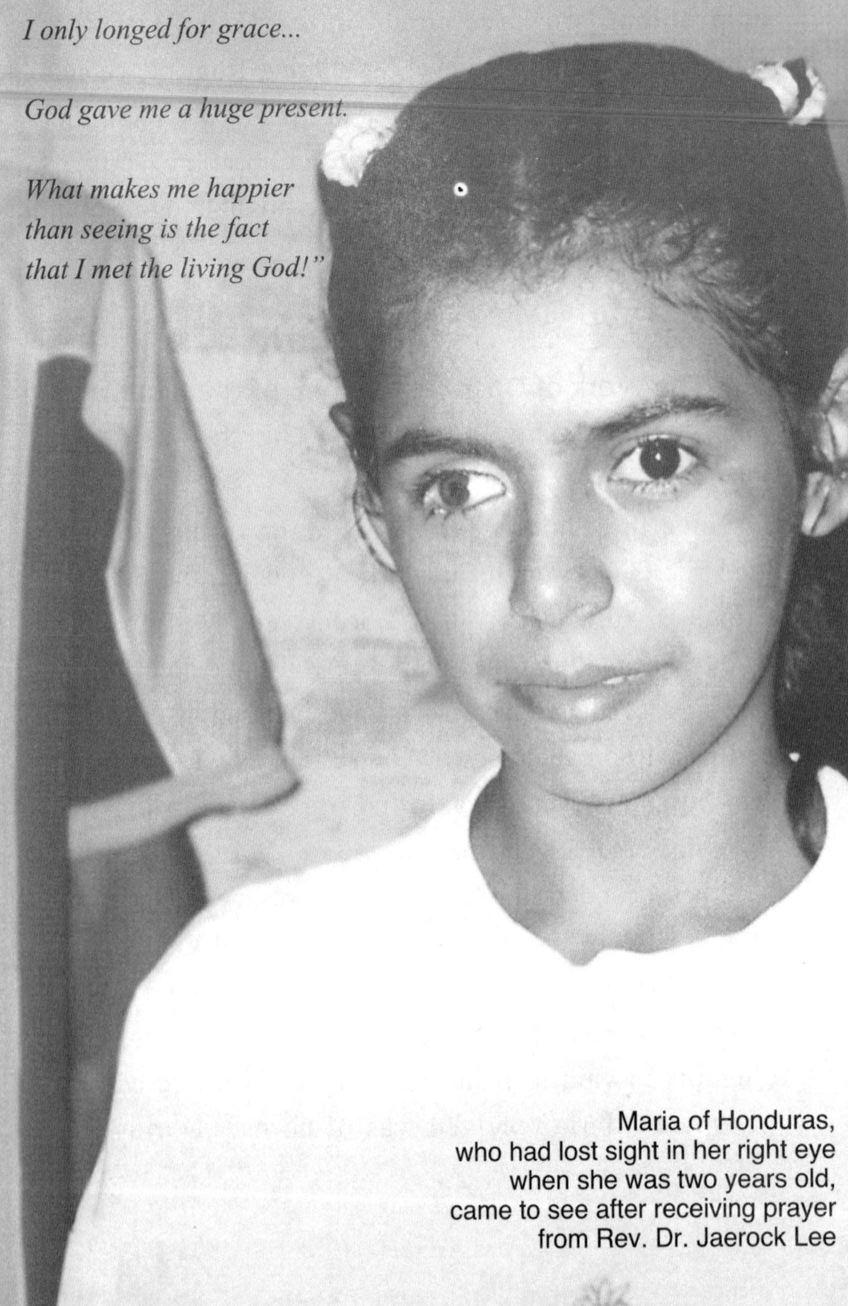

Maria of Honduras,
who had lost sight in her right eye
when she was two years old,
came to see after receiving prayer
from Rev. Dr. Jaerock Lee

following decade after the failure of the transplant, Maria could not even see light through her right eye. Then in 2002, in earnest desire for the grace of God, Maria attended the crusade at which she received my prayer, began to see the light, and was soon restored of her sight. Nerves in her right eye that had thoroughly failed and died were recreated by the power of God. How amazing is this? An immeasurable number of people in Honduras celebrated and exclaimed, "God is indeed alive and at work even today!"

Pastor Ricardo Morales had almost become blind but was healed completely by Muan sweet water. Seven years prior to the Honduras Crusade, Pastor Ricardo had been in a traffic accident in which his retina was critically damaged and suffered from severe hemorrhage. Doctors had told Pastor Ricardo that he would gradually lose his sight and ultimately become blind. Yet, he was healed on the first day of the 2002 Conference for Church Leaders in Honduras. After hearing the Word of God, in faith Pastor Ricardo put Muan sweet water on his eyes and much to his astonishment, objects became clearer by the minute. At first, because he had not anticipated anything like this, Pastor Ricardo could not believe it. That evening, with his glasses on, Pastor Ricardo attended the

"Doctors told me
I would soon be blind...
things began to fade...

Thank you, Lord,
for giving me the light...

I have been waiting for You..."

Rev. Ricardo Morales of Honduras,
who almost became blind after an accident
but has come to see

first session of the crusade. Then, all of a sudden, the lens from his eyeglasses came off and he heard the voice of the Holy Spirit: "If you do not take your glasses off now, you will be blind." Pastor Ricardo then took off his glasses and realized that he could see all things clearly. His sight was restored, and Pastor Ricardo greatly glorified God.

At the Nairobi Manmin Church in Kenya, a young man named Kombo once visited his hometown, which is about 400 kilometers (about 250 miles) from the church. During the visit, he spread the gospel to his family and told them of the wondrous work of God's power taking place at Manmin Joong-ang Church in Seoul. He prayed for them with the handkerchief on which I had prayed. Kombo also presented his family with a calendar printed by the church.

After hearing her grandson preach the gospel, Kombo's grandmother, who had been blind, thought to herself in earnest desire, 'I'd like to see a photograph of Rev. Dr. Jaerock Lee, too,' as she held the calendar with her two hands. What ensued was truly miraculous. As soon as Kombo's grandmother unfolded the calendar, her eyes opened and she could see the photograph. Hallelujah! Kombo's family had a firsthand experience of the work of power that opened the eyes of the blind and came to believe in the living God. Furthermore, when the news of this incident spread throughout the village, people asked for a branch church to be established in their village as well.

By the countless works of power all over the world, there are now thousands of Manmin branch churches worldwide, and the gospel of holiness is being preached to the ends of the earth. When you acknowledge and believe in the work of God's power, you can also become an heir to His blessings.

As it was the case during Jesus' time, instead of rejoicing and glorifying God together, many people today judge, condemn, and speak against the work of the Holy Spirit. We must realize that this is a frightful sin, as Jesus specifically told us in Matthew 12:31-32: *"And so I tell you, every sin and blasphemy will be forgiven men, but the blasphemy against the Spirit will not be forgiven. Anyone who speaks a word against the Son of Man will be forgiven, but anyone who speaks against the Holy Spirit will not be forgiven, either in this age or in the age to come."*

In order not to oppose the work of the Holy Spirit but instead experience the amazing work of God's power, we must acknowledge and long for His work, like the man who was blind in John 9. According to how much people have prepared themselves as vessels to receive answers by faith, some will experience the work of God's power while others will not.

As Psalm 18:25-26 tell us, *"To the faithful you show yourself faithful, to the blameless you show yourself blameless, to the pure you show yourself pure, but to the crooked you show yourself shrewd,"* may each of you, by believing in God who rewards us according to what you have done and displaying your deeds of faith, become an heir to His blessings, in the name of our Lord Jesus Christ I pray!

Message 7

People Will Get Up, Leap, and Walk

Mark 2:3-12

Some men came, bringing to him a paralytic,
carried by four of them.
Since they could not get him to Jesus
because of the crowd, they made an opening
in the roof above Jesus and, after digging through it,
lowered the mat the paralyzed man was lying on.
When Jesus saw their faith, he said to the paralytic,
"Son, your sins are forgiven."
Now some teachers of the law were sitting there,
thinking to themselves,
"Why does this fellow talk like that?
He's blaspheming! Who can forgive sins but
God alone?" Immediately Jesus knew in his spirit that
this was that they were thinking in their hearts,
and he said to them, "Why are you thinking these
things? Which is easier: to say to the paralytic,
'Your sins are forgiven,' or to say,
'Get up, take your mat and walk'?
But that you may know that the Son of Man has
authority on earth to forgive sins...."
He said to the paralytic, "I tell you, get up,
take your mat and go home."
He got up, took his mat and walked out in full view of
them all. This amazed everyone and
they praised God, saying, "We have never seen anything
like this!"

The Bible tells us that during the time of Jesus, many who had been paralyzed or crippled received complete healing and greatly glorified God. As God promised us in Isaiah 35:6, *"Then will the lame leap like a deer,"* and again in Isaiah 49:8, *"This is what the LORD says: 'In the time of my favor I will answer you, and in the day of salvation I will help you,'"* God will not only answer us but also lead us to salvation.

This is being testified unceasingly today at Manmin Joong-ang Church, where by the work of God's wondrous power countless patients begin walking, getting up from wheelchairs and throwing away their crutches.

With what kind of faith did the paralytic featured in Mark 2 come before Jesus and receive salvation and blessings of answers? I pray that those of you who are currently unable to walk due to some illness get up, walk, and run again.

The Paralytic Hears News about Jesus

In Mark 2 is a detailed account of a paralytic who received healing from Jesus when He visited Capernaum.

In that town lived a very poor paralytic who was unable to sit up on his own without the aid of others, and alive only because he could not die. Yet, he heard news about Jesus who had opened the eyes of the blind, had the crippled stand up, driven out evil spirits, and healed people of various kinds of diseases. For the man had a good heart, when he heard news about Jesus, he remembered them and came to earnestly desire to meet Jesus.

One day, the paralytic heard that Jesus had come to Capernaum. How excited and joyous must he have been in anticipation of meeting Jesus? The paralytic, however, was unable to move on his own, and thus sought friends who could bring him to Jesus. Luckily, because his friends had also been well aware of Jesus, they agreed to help their friend.

The Paralytic and His Friends Come before Jesus

The paralytic and his friends arrived at the house in which Jesus was preaching, but because there gathered a large crowd, they could not find any room near the door, much less go inside the house. The circumstances did not allow the paralytic and his friends to go before Jesus. They must have pleaded with the crowd, "Please move aside! We have a critically ill patient!" Nonetheless, the house and the vicinity were packed with people. If the paralytic and his friends had lacked faith, they might have returned home without meeting Jesus.

However, they did not give up but instead showed their faith. After pondering how they could meet Jesus, as the last resort the paralytic's friends began making a hole in the roof above Jesus and dug through it. Even if they were to apologize to the owner of the house and pay him for the damage at a later time, the paralytic and his friends were that desperate to meet Jesus and receive healing.

Faith is accompanied by deed, and the deeds of faith can be displayed only when you lower yourself with a humble heart. Have you ever thought or said to yourself, "Though I want to, my physical condition does not allow me to go to church"? If the paralytic had confessed a hundred times, "Lord, I believe that you know I cannot come to meet you because I am paralyzed. I also believe that you will heal me even as I lie on my bed," he would not have been said to have displayed his faith.

No matter what it was to cost him, the paralytic went before Jesus to receive healing. The paralytic believed and was convinced that he would be healed when he met Jesus, and he asked his friends to carry him before Jesus. Furthermore, since their friends also had faith, they could serve their paralyzed friend even by creating a hole and digging through a stranger's roof.

If you truly believe that you will be healed before God, coming before Him is an evidence of your faith. That is why after they dug through the roof, the paralytic's friends lowered the mat the paralyzed man was lying on and presented him before Jesus. At the time, roofs in Israel were flat and there was a staircase alongside each house that gave people easy access to the rooftop. Moreover, roof tiles could be easily removed. These accommodations permitted the paralytic to go before Jesus closer than anyone else.

We Can Receive Answers After We Solve the Problem of Sin

In Mark 2:5, we find that Jesus is evidently delighted with the deeds of faith of the paralytic. Before He healed the paralyzed man, why did Jesus tell him, "Son, your sins are forgiven"? This is because forgiveness of sins must precede healing.

In Exodus 15:26, God tells us, *"If you listen carefully to the voice of the LORD your God and do what is right in his eyes, if you pay attention to his commands and keep all his decrees, I will not bring on you any of the diseases I brought on the Egyptians, for I am the LORD, who heals you."* Here, "the diseases I brought on the Egyptians" refer to every disease known to man. Thus, when we obey His commands and live by His Word, God will protect us so that no disease can ever seize us. Moreover, in Deuteronomy 28 God promises us that so long as we obey and live by His Word, no disease will ever infiltrate our bodies. In John 5, after healing a man who had been ill for thirty-eight years, Jesus told him, "Stop sinning or something worse may happen to you" (v. 14).

For all diseases stem from sin, before He healed the paralytic Jesus first gave him forgiveness. Going before Jesus, however, does not always result in forgiveness. In order to receive healing, we must first repent of our sins and turn our ways from them. If you were a sinner, you must become one who no longer sins; if you were a liar, you must become one who no longer lies; and if you hated others, you must no longer hate. Only to those who obey the Word does God give forgiveness. Moreover, confessing "I believe" does not grant you forgiveness; when we come out to the light, the blood of our Lord will naturally cleanse us from all our sins (1 John 1:7).

The Paralytic Walks by the Power of God

In Mark 2:12, we find that after receiving forgiveness, the man who had been paralyzed got up, took his mat and walked out in full view of all the people there. When he came to Jesus, he was lying on a mat. The man was healed, however, the moment Jesus told him, "Son, your sins are forgiven." Instead of rejoicing over the healing, however, the teachers of the law were busy quarreling. When Jesus told the man, "Son, your sins are forgiven," they thought to themselves, "Why does this fellow talk like that? He's blaspheming! Who can forgive sins but God alone?"

Then Jesus told them, "Why are you thinking these things? Which is easier: to say to the paralytic, 'Your sins are forgiven,' or to say, 'Get up, take your mat and walk'? But that you may know that the Son of Man has authority on earth to forgive sins." After enlightening them on the providence of God, when Jesus told the paralytic, "I tell you, get up, take your mat and go home," the man immediately got up and walked. In other words, for the man who had been paralyzed to receive healing indicates that he received forgiveness, and that God guaranteed every word Jesus spoke. It is also the evidence that the omnipotent God guarantees Jesus as the Savior of mankind.

Instances of Getting Up, Leaping, and Walking at Manmin

In John 14:11, Jesus tells us, *"Believe me when I say that I am in the Father and the Father is in me; or at least believe on the evidence of the miracles themselves."* Therefore, we are to believe that Father God and Jesus are one and the same by witnessing that the paralytic who came before Jesus in faith was forgiven, got up, leaped and walked at Jesus' command.

In the following John 14:12, Jesus also tells us, *"I tell you the truth, anyone who has faith in me will do what I have been doing. He will do even greater things than these, because I am going to the Father."* As I believed the Word of God one-hundred percent, after I was called as a servant of God I fasted and prayed many, many days to receive His power. Consequently, testimonies of healings of diseases modern medical science could not handle have been overflowing at Manmin since its founding.

Each time the church as a whole passed trials of blessings, the speed at which patients received healing quickened while more critical diseases were healed. Through the annual Two-week Special Revival Meeting held from 1993 to 2004 and worldwide Great United Crusades, a great number of people all over the world have experienced the astonishing power of God.

Among countless instances in which people have gotten up, leapt, and walked, here are a few examples.

Standing Up After Nine Years in the Wheelchair

The first testimony is of Deacon Yoonsup Kim. In May 1990, he fell from the height of about a five-story building while doing electrical work at the Taedok Science Town in South Korea. This happened before Kim came to believe in God.

Immediately after the fall, he was taken to the Sun Hospital in Yoosung, Choongnam Province, where he was in coma for six months. After waking up from the coma, however, the pain of pressure and rupture in 11th and 12th thoracic vertebrae and hernia in 4th and 5th lumbar vertebrae was unbearably agonizing. Doctors at the hospital informed Kim that his condition was critical. He was admitted to other hospitals a number of times. However, without any change or progress in his condition,

Kim was found to be of the first-degree disability. Around his waist, Kim was to wear a brace for his spine at all times. Moreover, since he could not lie down he had to sleep while sitting up.

During this difficult time, Kim was evangelized and came to Manmin, where he began a life in Christ. When he attended the Special Meeting for Divine Healing in November 1998, Kim had an unbelievable experience. Prior to the Meeting, he was unable to lie down on his back or use the restroom on his own. After receiving my prayer, he could get up from his wheelchair and walk on crutches.

In order to receive complete healing, Deacon Kim faithfully attended all worship services and meetings and never stopped praying. In addition, in earnest desire and preparation for the 7th Two-week Special Revival Meeting in May 1999, he fasted for twenty-one days. When I prayed for the sick from the pulpit during the first session of the Meeting, Deacon Kim felt a strong ray of light shining on him and saw a vision in which he was running. In the second week of the Meeting, when I laid my hands on and prayed for him, he could feel that his body was lighter. When the fire of the Holy Spirit descended on his feet, strength unknown to him was given. He could throw away his spine-supporting brace

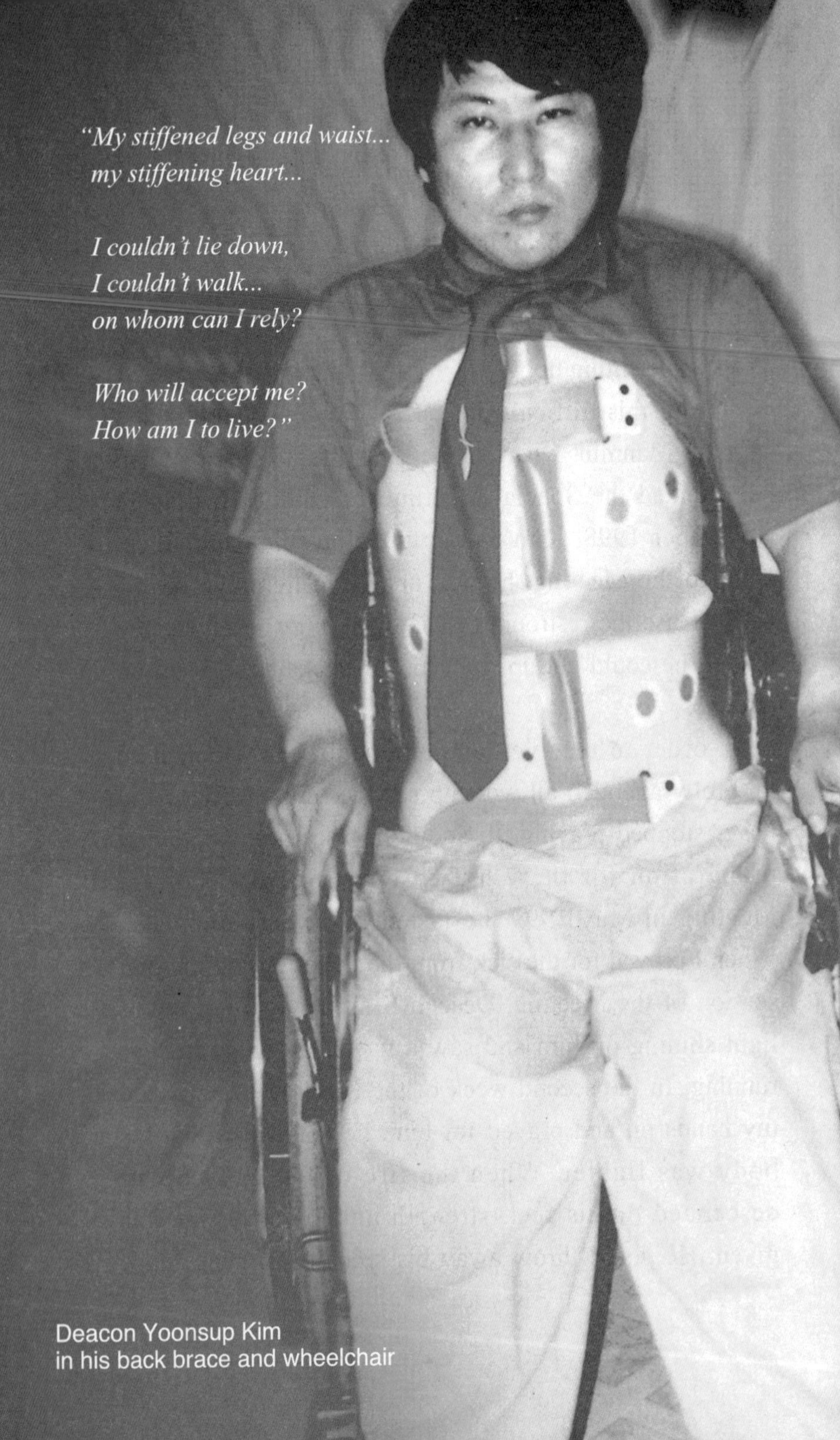

"My stiffened legs and waist...
my stiffening heart...

I couldn't lie down,
I couldn't walk...
on whom can I rely?

Who will accept me?
How am I to live?"

Deacon Yoonsup Kim
in his back brace and wheelchair

*"Hallelujah!
God is alive!
Can you see me walking?"*

Deacon Kim rejoices with other Manmin members after receiving healing through the prayer of Rev. Dr. Jaerock Lee

and crutches, walk without any difficulty, and freely move his waist.

By the power of God, Deacon Kim has come to walk as an ordinary person. He even rides his bicycle and diligently serves at the church. Moreover, not long ago Deacon Kim has gotten married and is now leading a truly happy life.

Getting Up from the Wheelchair after Receiving Handkerchief Prayer

At Manmin, spectacular events that are recorded in the Bible and extraordinary miracles take place; through them God is glorified even further. Among such events and miracles is the manifestation of God's power through handkerchiefs.

In Acts 19:11-12, we find that *"God did extraordinary miracles through Paul, so that even handkerchiefs and aprons that had touched him were taken to the sick, and their illnesses were cured and the evil spirits left them."* Likewise, when people take the handkerchiefs on which I prayed or any objects on my body to the sick, wondrous work of healing is manifested. As a consequence, many countries and peoples all over the world have asked us to conduct handkerchief crusades in their own regions. Furthermore, countless people in countries in Africa, Pakistan, Indonesia, the Philippines, Honduras, Japan, China, Russia, and many others are experiencing "extraordinary miracles" as well.

In April 2001, one of Manmin's pastors conducted a handkerchief crusade in Indonesia, at which countless people received healing and gave glory to the living God. Among them was a former state governor, who had relied on a wheelchair. When he was healed after handkerchief prayer, it soon became a big news story.

In May 2003, another pastor of Manmin conducted a handkerchief crusade in China at which, among many instances of healing, a man who had relied on crutches for thirty-four years came to walk on his own.

Ganesh Throws Away His Crutches at the 2002 Great United Crusade in India

At the 2002 India Great United Crusade, which took place on the Marina Beach in Chennai of predominantly-Hindu India, more than three million people gathered, witnessed firsthand truly astonishing work of the power of God, and many of them converted to Christianity. Prior to this crusade, the pace at which stiffened bones became loose and dead nerves revived had progressed slowly. Beginning with the India Crusade, the work of healing defied the order of the human body.

Among those who received healing were a sixteen-year-old boy named Ganesh. He had fallen from his bicycle and hurt his right pelvis. Difficult financial situations at home had prevented him from receiving proper treatment. After a year passed, a tumor developed in his bone and he was forced to have his right pelvis removed. Doctors installed a thin metal board on his thighbone and remaining portions of his pelvis, and fastened the board with nine nails. The excruciating pain from the fastened nails made it impossible for him to walk up and down a staircase or walk without crutches.

When he heard about the crusade, he attended it and experienced the fiery work of the Holy Spirit. On the second of the four-day crusade, as he received the "Prayer for the Sick" he felt his body heat up, as though it was placed in a pot of boiling water, and no longer felt any pain in his body. He immediately went up to the stage and gave a testimony of his healing. Thenceforth, he has felt no pain anywhere in his body, not used crutches, and come to freely walk and run.

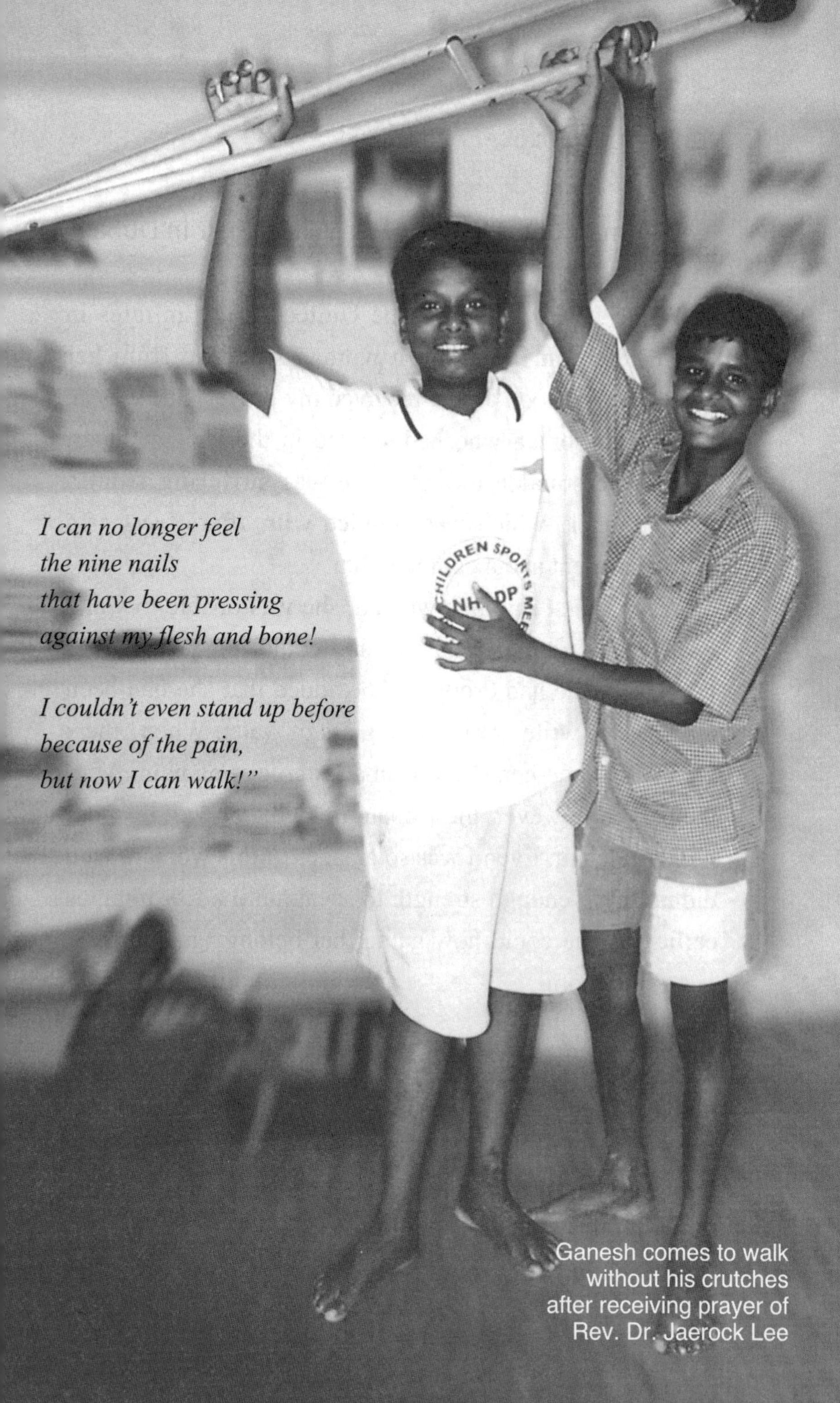
I can no longer feel
the nine nails
that have been pressing
against my flesh and bone!

I couldn't even stand up before
because of the pain,
but now I can walk!"

Ganesh comes to walk without his crutches after receiving prayer of Rev. Dr. Jaerock Lee

A Woman Gets Up from Her Wheelchair in Dubai

While I was in Dubai, the United Arab Emirates in April 2003, an Indian-born woman stood up from her wheelchair as soon as she received my prayer. She was an intelligent woman who had studied in the United States. Due to personal problems, she was suffering from a mental shock, which was coupled with aftereffects of a traffic accident and a complication.

When I first saw this woman, she was unable to walk, lacked the strength to speak, and could not pick up her eyeglasses she had dropped. She added that she had been too weak to write or pick up a glass of water. When others merely touched her, she was in an excruciating pain. After the prayer, however, the woman immediately got up from her wheelchair. Even I was so amazed at this woman, who did not have enough strength to speak until a few minutes earlier, as she could now gather her belongings and walk out of the room.

Jeremiah 29:11 tells us, *"'For I know the plans I have for you,' declares the LORD, 'plans to prosper you and not to harm you, plans to give you hope and a future.'"* Our Father God has loved us so much that He has unsparingly given His one and only Son.

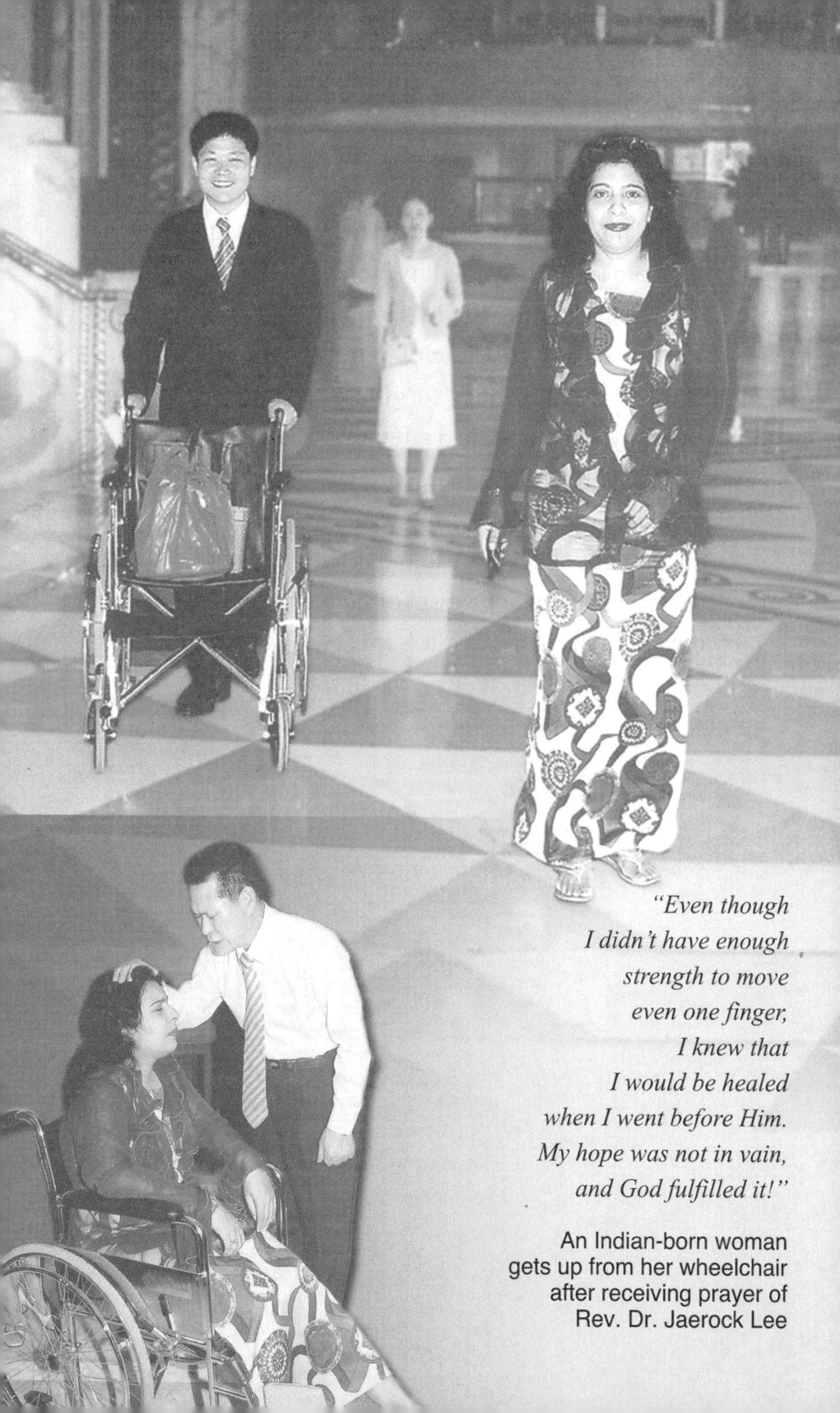

"Even though I didn't have enough strength to move even one finger, I knew that I would be healed when I went before Him. My hope was not in vain, and God fulfilled it!"

An Indian-born woman gets up from her wheelchair after receiving prayer of Rev. Dr. Jaerock Lee

Therefore, even if you have been living a miserable life because of physical disability, you have the hope of living a happy and healthy life by the faith in God. He does not want to see any of His children in trials and affliction. Furthermore, He longs to give everyone in the world peace, joy, happiness, and a future.

Through the story of a paralytic featured in Mark 2, you have come to know the ways and methods by which you can receive answers to the desires of your heart. May each of you prepare a vessel of faith and receive whatever you ask, in the name of our Lord Jesus Christ I pray!

Message 8

People Will Rejoice, Dance, and Sing

Mark 7:31-37

Then Jesus left the vicinity of Tyre
and went through Sidon,
down to the Sea of Galilee
and into the region of the Decapolis.
There some people brought to him a man
who was deaf and could hardly talk,
and they begged him to place his hand on the man.
After he took him aside, away from the crowd,
Jesus put his fingers into the man's ears.
Then he spit and touched the man's tongue.
He looked up to heaven and with a deep sigh said to him,
"Ephphatha!" (which means, "Be opened!").
At this, the man's ears were opened,
his tongue was loosened and he began to speak plainly.
Jesus commanded them not to tell anyone.
But the more he did so, the more they kept talking about it.
People were overwhelmed with amazement.
"He has done everything well," they said.
"He even makes the deaf hear and the mute speak."

We find the following in Matthew 4:23-24:

Jesus went throughout Galilee, teaching in their synagogues, preaching the good news of the kingdom, and healing every disease and sickness among the people. News about him spread all over Syria, and people brought to him all who were ill with various diseases, those suffering severe pain, the demon-possessed, those having seizures, and the paralyzed, and he healed them.

Jesus not only preached the Word of God and the good news of the kingdom, but also healed countless people suffering from a variety of diseases. By healing diseases to which man's power was useless, the Word Jesus proclaimed was engraved in the hearts of people, and He led them to heaven by their faith.

Jesus Heals a Deaf and Mute Man

In Mark 7 is a story about the time Jesus traveled from Tyre to Sidon, then from there to the Sea of Galilee and into the region of the Decapolis, and healed a deaf and mute man. If someone "could hardly talk," that means he stuttered and could not speak eloquently. The man from this passage probably learned to speak when he was a child, but became deaf later, and "could hardly talk" now.

By and large, a "deaf-mute" is someone who has not learned the language and to speak because of the deafness, while "bradyacusia" refers to the difficulty in hearing. There are a number of ways in which one becomes a deaf-mute. The first of these is hereditary. In the second case, one becomes an inborn deaf-mute if the mother suffers from rubella (otherwise known as "German measles") or takes wrong medication during the pregnancy. In the third case, if the child is diagnosed with meningitis when he is three or four years old, at a time a child learns to speak, one can become a deaf-mute. In the case of bradyacusia, if the eardrum has been ruptured, hearing aids can ease the difficulty. If there is a problem in the auditory nerve itself, no hearing aid will help. For other cases in which one works in a very noisy setting or the weakening of hearing occurs as one advances in age, there is said to be no fundamental cure.

In addition, one can become deaf or mute if he is demon-possessed. In such a case, when an individual with spiritual authority drives out demons, the person will come to hear and speak immediately. When Jesus rebuked an evil spirit in a boy who had been unable to speak, "You deaf and mute spirit, I command you, come out of him and never enter him again," the evil spirit left the boy at once and the boy became well (Mark 9:25-27).

Believe that when God works, no disease and infirmities will ever pose a problem or threat to you. That is why we find in Jeremiah 32:27, *"I am the LORD, the God of all mankind. Is anything too hard for me?"* Psalm 100:3 urges us to *"Know that the LORD is God. It is he who made us, and we are his; we are his people, the sheep of his pasture,"* while Psalm 94:9 reminds us, *"Does he who implanted the ear not hear? Does he who formed the eye not see?"* When we believe in the omnipotent Father God who formed our ears and eyes from the bottom of our hearts, everything is possible. That is why for Jesus, who came to the earth in flesh, everything was possible. As we find in Mark 7, when Jesus healed the deaf and mute man, the man's ears were opened and His words became coherent.

When we do not only believe in Jesus Christ but also ask for God's power with matured faith, the same work as recorded in the Bible will take place even today. On this,

Hebrews 13:8 tells us, *"Jesus Christ is the same yesterday and today and forever,"* while Ephesians 4:13 reminds us that we are to *"reach unity in the faith and in the knowledge of the Son of God and become mature, attaining to the whole measure of the fullness of Christ."*

However, degeneration of body parts or deafness and muteness as a result of the death of nerve cells cannot be cured by the gift of healing. Only when an individual, who has attained to the whole measure of the fullness of Jesus Christ, receives the power and authority from God and prays in accordance with the will of God, will the healing take place.

Instances of God's Healing of Deafness at Manmin

I have witnessed many instances in which bradyacusia was healed, and countless people who had once been unable to hear since birth coming to hear for the first time. There are two people who have come to hear for the first time in 55 and 57 years.

In September 2000, when I conducted a Miracle Healing Festival in Nagoya, Japan, thirteen people who had been suffering from hearing impairment received healing as soon as they received my prayer. This news

A song of thanksgiving by the people who has been healed of their deafness

"With the lives
You have given us,

we will walk
on the earth
in longing for You.

My soul that is as clear
as crystal comes to You."

Deaconess Napshim Park gives glory to God after having been healed of the 55-year deafness

was relayed back to many of the hearing impaired in Korea, and many of them attended the 9th Two-week Special Revival Meeting in May 2001, received healing, and greatly glorified God.

Among them was a 33-year-old woman, who had been a deaf-mute since an accident when she was eight years old. After having been led to our church shortly before the 2001 Meeting, she prepared herself to receive answers. The woman attended the daily "Daniel Night Prayer Meeting" and, as she remembered her sins of the past, she rent her heart. After preparing herself for the Revival Meeting in earnest desire, she attended the Meeting. During the last session of the Meeting, when I laid my hand on deaf-mutes to pray for them, she felt no immediate change. Nonetheless, she was not disappointed. Instead, she saw the testimonies of those who had received healing in rejoicing and gratitude, and believed even more earnestly that she, too, could be healed.

God deemed this as faith and healed the woman shortly after the Meeting ended. I have seen the work of God's power manifested even after the Meeting concluded. Moreover, the hearing test she underwent only testified to complete healing in both ears. Hallelujah!

Inborn Deafness Receives Healing

The magnitude of the manifestation of God's power has increased year after year. At the 2002 Honduras Great United Crusade, countless people who had been deaf and mute came to hear and speak. When the daughter of the head of the security personnel during the crusade was healed of her lifelong deafness, she became so excited and exceedingly grateful.

One of the ears of an eight-year-old Madeline Yaimin Bartres had not grown properly and she had gradually lost hearing. Upon hearing about the crusade, Madeline begged her father to take her to it. She received abundant grace during praise time, and after receiving my prayer, she began to hear clearly. As her father worked faithfully for the crusade, God blessed his child in this manner.

At the 2002 India Great United Crusade, Jennifer Removes Her Hearing Aid

Although we were unable to register all the countless testimonies of healing during and after the India Crusade, even with a selected few we are compelled to give thanks and glory to God. Among such cases is the story of a girl named Jennifer, who had been deaf and mute since birth. A doctor suggested that she wear hearing aids which would improve her hearing a little, but reminded her that the hearing could not be perfect.

While Jennifer's mother prayed everyday for her daughter's healing, they attended the crusade. The mother and daughter sat nearby one of the large speakers because the proximity to the loud speaker would not have troubled Jennifer anyway. On the last day of the crusade, however, because of the larger crowd that gathered, they could not find seats near the speaker. What ensued was truly unbelievable. As soon as I completed the prayer for the sick from the pulpit, Jennifer told her mother that all the sound was too loud and asked her mother to remove the hearing aids. Hallelujah!

According to medical records prior to the healing, without the hearing aids, Jennifer's hearing would not respond to even the highest intensity of the sound. In other words, Jennifer had lost one-hundred percentage of her hearing, but after the prayer it was found that 30~50 percentage of her hearing had been renewed. The following is otorhinolaryngologist Christina's evaluation of Jennifer:

In order to assess the hearing ability of Jennifer,

Jennifer, healed of her born deafness
and her doctor's evaluation

CHURCH OF SOUTH INDIA

Phone : 857 11 01
859 23 06

MADRAS DIOCESE

C. S. I. KALYANI MULTI SPECIALITY HOSPITAL

15, Dr. Radhakrishnan Salai, Chennai-600 004. (South India)

Ref. No.

Date 15/10/02

To whom it may concern.

Miss Jennifer aged 5 yrs has been examined by me at CSI Kalyani hospital for her hearing.

After interacting with the child and observing her and after examining this child, I have come to the conclusion that Jennifer has definitely good hearing improvement now than before she was prayed for. Her mother's observation of ~~her~~ child is far more important and the mother has definitely noticed marked improvement in her child's hearing ability: Jennifer hears much better without the hearing aid, responding to her name being called, where as previously she was not, without the aid.

Audiogram Result: Moderate to Severe sensori-neural hearing loss i.e 50% – 70% hearing loss.
Christie

Christie
ENT Surgeon.

Medical Officer,
C. S. I. KALYANI GENERAL HOSPITAL
Mylapore, Chennai.

KALYANI HOSPITAL

> age 5, I examined her at C.S.I. Kalyani Multi Specialty Hospital. After speaking with Jennifer and examining her, I reached a conclusion that there had been a certain and remarkable improvement in her hearing after the prayer. Opinions of Jennifer's mother are also pertinent. She made the same observation I had made: Jennifer's hearing had certainly and drastically improved. At this time, Jennifer can hear well without any hearing aids and responds well when people call her name. This wasn't the case without the hearing aids prior to the prayer.

To those who prepare their hearts in faith, the power of God is without doubt manifested. Of course, there are many instances in which patients' conditions improve day by day so long as they lead faithful lives in Christ.

Oftentimes, God does not give complete healing at first to those who have been deaf from the time they were young. If they could come to hear well from the moment they were healed, it would be difficult for them to withstand all the sounds. If people lost hearing after they had grown up, God may heal them completely right away because it will not take as much time for them to adjust to the sounds. In such cases, people may be confused at first but after a day or two, they will be calm and become accustomed to their ability to hear.

In April 2003, during my trip to Dubai, I met a 32-year-old woman who had lost speech after suffering from cerebral meningitis when she was two years old. As soon as she received my prayer, very clearly the woman said, "Thank you!" I thought of her remark only as a token of appreciation, but her parents told me that three decades had passed since their daughter last uttered, "Thank you."

In Order to Experience the Power That Enables the Mute to Speak and the Deaf to Hear

In Mark 7:33-35 is the following:

> *After he took him aside, away from the crowd, Jesus put his fingers into the man's ears. Then he spit and touched the man's tongue. He looked up to heaven and with a deep sigh said to him, "Ephphatha!" (which means, "Be opened!"). At this, the man's ears were opened, his tongue was loosened and he began to speak plainly."*

Here, "Ephphatha" means "Open" in Hebrew. When

Jesus commanded in the original voice of creation, the man's ears were opened and his tongue was loosened.

Why, then, did Jesus put His fingers into the man's ears prior to commanding, "Ephphatha"? Romans 10:17 tells us, *"Consequently, faith comes from hearing the message, and the message is heard through the word of Christ."* Since this man could not hear, it was not easy for him to possess faith.

Furthermore, the man did not come before Jesus to receive healing. Instead, some people brought this man to Jesus. By putting His fingers into the man's ears, Jesus helped the man to possess faith through the sense of His fingers.

Only when we understand the spiritual meaning embedded in the scene in which Jesus manifested God's power, can we experience His power. What specific steps are we to take?

We must first possess the faith to receive healing.

Even if it is little, the one who needs to receive healing must possess faith. However, unlike the times of Jesus and because of the advancement of civilization, there are many mediums, including sign language, by which even the hearing-impaired can come across the gospel.

Beginning a few years ago, all sermon messages have been simultaneously translated in sign language at Manmin. The messages from the past are also being continuously updated in sign language on its website as well.

Furthermore, by many other ways, including books, newspapers, magazines, and video and audio cassette tapes, you can possess faith so long as you have the resolve. Once faith is attained, you can experience the power of God. I have mentioned a number of testimonies as a means to help you possess faith.

Next, we must receive forgiveness.

Why did Jesus spit and touch the man's tongue after He had put his fingers in the man's ears? This spiritually symbolizes baptism by water and was necessary for the forgiveness of the man's sins. Baptism by water means that by the Word of God that is like clean water, we are to be cleansed from all our sins. In order to experience the power of God, one must first solve the problem of sin. Instead of cleansing the man's uncleanness by water, Jesus substituted it with His saliva, and symbolized thus forgiveness of this man. Isaiah 59:1-2 tell us, *"Surely the arm of the LORD is not too short to save, nor his ear too dull to hear. But your iniquities have separated you from your God; your sins have hidden his face from you, so that he will not hear."*

As God promised us in 2 Chronicles 7:14, *"[If] my people, who are called by my name, will humble themselves and pray and seek my face and turn from their wicked ways, then will I hear from heaven and will forgive their sin and will heal their land,"* in order to receive answers before God, you must look back at yourself truthfully, rend your heart, and repent.

Of what should we repent before God?

First, you must repent of not having believed in God and accepted Jesus Christ. In John 16:9, Jesus tells us that the Holy Spirit will convict the world of guilt in regard to sin, because men do not believe in Jesus. You must realize that not accepting the Lord is a sin, and thus believe in the Lord and God.

Second, if you have not loved your brothers, you must repent. 1 John 4:11 tells us, *"Dear friends, since God so loved us, we also ought to love one another."* If your brother hates you, instead of hating him in return, you must be tolerant and forgiving. You must also love your enemy, seek first his benefits, and think and behave as you place yourself in his shoes. When you come to love all people, God will also show you compassion, mercy, and the work of healing.

Third, if you have prayed for self-interests, you must repent. God does not delight in those who pray with selfish motives. He will not answer you. Even from now on, you must pray in accordance with the will of God.

Fourth, if you have prayed but doubted, you must repent. James 1:6-7 read, *"But when he asks, he must believe and not doubt, because he who doubts is like a wave of the sea, blown and tossed by the wind. That man should not think he will receive anything from the Lord."* Accordingly, when we pray, we must pray by faith and please Him. Moreover, as Hebrews 11:6 reminds us, *"without faith it is impossible to please God,"* throw away your doubts and ask only by faith.

Fifth, if you have not obeyed God's commands, you must repent. As Jesus in John 14:21 tells us, *"Whoever has my commands and obeys them, he is the one who loves me,"* when you display the proof of your love for God by obeying His commands, you can receive answers from Him. From time to time, believers are involved in traffic accidents. That is because most of them have not kept the Lord's Day holy or offered their whole tithes. Since they did not abide by the most fundamental set of rules for Christians, the Ten Commandments, they could not be placed under God's protection. Among those who faithfully obey His commands, some of them do get involved in accidents by their own mistakes. Yet, they are protected by God. In such cases, the people inside remain unharmed even in a totaled vehicle, because God loves them and shows them the proof of His love.

Moreover, people who have not known God often receive quick healing after receiving prayer. This is because the fact that they came to the church itself is a deed of faith, and God works in them. However, when people have faith and know the truth but keep on disobeying God's commands and do not live by His Word, this becomes a wall between God and those people, and hence they cannot receive healing. The reason God works greatly among nonbelievers during overseas Great United Crusades is because the fact that those who worship idols hear the news and attended the crusades itself is deemed faith in the sight of God.

Sixth, if you have not sowed, you must repent. As

Galatians 6:7 tells us, *"A man reaps what he sows,"* in order to experience God's power, you must first attend worship services diligently. Remember that when you sow with your body, you will receive blessings of health, and when you sow with your wealth, you will receive blessings of wealth. Thus, if you have wanted to reap without sowing, you must repent of that.

1 John 1:7 reads, *"But if we walk in the light, as he is in the light, we have fellowship with one another, and the blood of Jesus, his Son, purifies us from all sin."* Moreover, holding fast to God's promise in 1 John 1:9, *"If we confess our sins, he is faithful and just and will forgive us our sins and purify us from all unrighteousness,"* be sure to look back at yourself, repent, and walk in the light.

May you receive God's compassion, receive everything you ask, and by His power receive not only blessings of health but also blessings in all affairs and matters in life, in the name of our Lord Jesus Christ I pray!

Message 9

The Unfailing Providence of God

Deuteronomy 26:16-19

The LORD your God commands
you this day to follow these decrees and laws;
carefully observe them with all your heart
and with all your soul.
You have declared this day that the LORD is your God
and that you will walk in his ways,
that you will keep his decrees,
commands and laws, and that you will obey him.
And the LORD has declared this day
that you are his people,
his treasured possession as he promised,
and that you are to keep all his commands.
He has declared that he will set you in praise,
fame and honor high above all the nations
he has made and that you will be a people
holy to the LORD your God, as he promised.

If asked to select the utmost form of love, many people will choose the love of parents, especially a mother's love for her infant child. Yet, we find in Isaiah 49:15, *"Can a mother forget the baby at her breast and have no compassion on the child she has borne? Though she may forget, I will not forget you!"* The abundant love of God is incomparable to the love of a mother for her infant child.

The God of love wants all the people to not only reach salvation, but also enjoy the eternal life, blessing, and pleasure in the magnificent heaven. That is why He delivers His children from trials and afflictions and wants to give everything they ask. God also leads each of us to live a blessed life not only on the earth, but in the eternal life that is to come as well.

Now, through power and prophecies God has permitted us in His love, we will examine the providence of God for Manmin Joong-ang Church.

The Love of God Wants to Save All Souls

We find the following in 2 Peter 3:3-4:

> *First of all, you must understand that in the last days scoffers will come, scoffing and following their own evil desires. They will say, "Where is this 'coming' he promised? Ever since our fathers died, everything goes on as it has since the beginning of creation."*

There are many people who would not believe us when we tell them of the end of the age. As the sun has always risen and set, as people have always been born and died, and as the civilization has always advanced, such people naturally assume that everything will go on and on.

As there are both a beginning and an end to a man's life, if there is a beginning in the history of mankind, there surely is an end to it. When the time of God's choosing arrives, everything in the universe will face an end. All the people who have ever lived since Adam will receive judgment. According to how one has lived on the earth, he will enter either heaven or hell.

On the one hand, people who believe in Jesus Christ and live by the Word of God will enter heaven. On the other hand, people who do not believe even after having been evangelized, and people who do not live by God's Word but instead live in sin and evil, even though they confess their faith in the Lord, will enter hell. That is why

God is eager to spread the gospel throughout the world as quickly as possible, so that even an additional soul may receive salvation.

The Power of God is Spread at the End of the Age

The very reason God has established Manmin Joong-ang Church and manifests wondrous power lies here. Through the manifestation of His power, God wants to provide evidence of the existence of a true God, and enlighten people on the reality of heaven and hell. As Jesus told us in John 4:48, *"Unless you people see miraculous signs and wonders, you will never believe,"* especially in a time in which sin and evil thrive and knowledge advances, the work of power that can shatter man's thought is all the more necessary. That is why, at the end of the age, God disciplines Manmin and blesses it with ever-growing power.

Moreover, the cultivation of mankind which God has designed is also approaching its end. Until the time of God's choosing arrives, power is a necessary device that can save all the people who have a chance of receiving salvation. Only with power can more people be led to salvation at a faster rate.

Due to persistent persecution and affliction, it is extremely difficult to spread the gospel in some countries around the world, and there are even more people who have not yet even heard of the gospel. Furthermore, even among those who profess their faith in the Lord, the number of people with true faith is not as high as people think. In Luke 18:8 Jesus asks us, *"However, when the Son of Man comes, will he find faith on the earth?"* Many people attend church, but without much difference from the people of the world, they continue to live in sin.

Yet, even in countries and regions of the world where there is severe persecution of Christianity, once the people experience the work of the power of God, the faith that does not fear death blossoms and the fiery spread of the gospel ensues. People who live in sin without true faith are now empowered to live by the Word of God when they experience firsthand the work of the power of the living God.

On many mission trips abroad, I have been to countries that legally prohibit evangelization and preaching of the gospel and persecute church. I have witnessed in such countries as Pakistan and the United Arab Emirates, in both of which Islam flourishes, and a predominantly Hindu state India, that when Jesus Christ is testified and evidences by which people could believe in the living

God are manifested, countless souls have converted and reached salvation. Even if they have worshiped idols, once they experience the work of the power of God, people come to accept Jesus Christ without fear of legal ramifications. This testifies to the sheer magnitude of the power of God.

As a farmer reaps his crops at harvest, God manifests such wondrous power so that He may reap all the souls who are to receive salvation in the last days.

Signs of the End of the Age Recorded in the Bible

Even by the Word of God recorded in the Bible, we can tell the time in which we live is close to the end of the age. Although God has not told us the exact date and time of the end of the age, He has given us clues by which we can tell of the end of the age. As we can predict that rain is imminent when the clouds start to gather, through the way in which the history continues to unfold itself, signs in the Bible allow us to predict the last days.

For instance, in Luke 21 we find, *"When you hear of wars and revolutions, do not be frightened"* (v. 9), and *"There will be great earthquakes, famines and pestilences in various places, and fearful events and great signs from heaven"* (v. 11). In 2 Timothy 3:1-5, we read the following:

> *But mark this: There will be terrible times in the last days. People will be lovers of themselves, lovers of money, boastful, proud, abusive, disobedient to their parents, ungrateful, unholy, without love, unforgiving, slanderous, without self-control, brutal, not lovers of the good, treacherous, rash, conceited, lovers of pleasure rather than lovers of God – having a form of godliness but denying its power. Have nothing to do with them.*

There are many disasters and signs all over the world, and the heart and thought of people are becoming more evil today. Every week, I receive a clipping of news stories on events and accidents, and the volume of each clipping has been steadily increasing. This means that there are that many disasters, calamities, and evildoings taking place in the world.

Yet, people are not as sensitive to these events and accidents as they have once been. Since they encounter too many stories of such events and accidents on a regular basis, people have become immune to them. Most of them no longer take seriously brutal crimes, great wars, natural disasters, and casualties from such atrocities and calamites. These events used to fill the headlines on mass media. However, unless they are deeply felt or occur to others they know, for most people such events are not that significant and soon become forgotten.

Through the way in which the history unfolds itself, people who are awake and have clear communication with God witness in one voice that the Advent of the Lord is imminent.

Prophecies on the End of the Age and God's Providence for Manmin Joong-ang Church

Through God's prophecies revealed to Manmin, we can tell it is indeed the end of the age. Since Manmin's founding to this day, God has foretold the results of presidential and parliamentary elections, deaths of important and well-known figures both in Korea and abroad, and many other events that have shaped the history of the world.

On many occasions I have disclosed such information in acronyms on weekly church bulletins. If the contents were too sensitive, I disclosed them only to a few individuals. In recent years, I have proclaimed from the pulpit from time to time revelations concerning North Korea, the United States, and events to take place worldwide.

Most of the prophecies have been fulfilled as foretold, and prophecies that are yet to be fulfilled concern events that are either on-going or that are still to come. A notable fact is that most of the prophecies concerning events that are still to come concern the last days. For among them are God's providence for Manmin Joong-ang Church, we will examine a few of these prophecies.

The first prophecy concerns the North and South Korean relations.

Since the founding, God has revealed a great deal on North Korea to Manmin. This is because we have a calling for evangelization of North Korea in the last days. In 1983, God foretold us of a summit between a North and a South Korean leaders and its aftermath. Soon after the summit, North Korea was to open its doors to the world temporarily but would close them again before long. God has told us that when North Korea opens up, the gospel of holiness and power of God would enter the country and evangelization would ensue. God told us to remember that the Advent of the Lord would be imminent when both North and South Koreas express themselves in a certain manner. For God has told me to keep the way the two Koreas would "express in a certain manner" a secret, I cannot yet divulge that information.

As most of you are aware, a summit between the leaders of the two Koreas took place in 2000. You could probably feel that North Korea, succumbing to international pressure, will open its doors before long.

The second prophecy concerns the calling for world mission.

God has prepared for Manmin a number of overseas crusades at which tens of thousands, hundreds of thousands, and millions of people gathered, and blessed us to quickly evangelize the world by His wondrous power. They include the Great United Crusade in Uganda, news of which was broadcast internationally on the Cable News Network (CNN); the Great United Crusade in Pakistan, which shook the Islamic world and opened the door for missionary work in the Middle East; the Great United Crusade in Kenya at which many, many diseases, including AIDS, have been healed; the Great United Crusade in the Philippines at which God's power was manifested explosively; the Great United Crusade in Honduras, which brought forth the Holy Spirit's hurricane; and the Great United Crusade in India, the largest Hindu country in the world, at which over three million people gathered during the four-day crusade. All these crusades have served as a steppingstone from which Manmin could enter Israel, its final destination.

Under His grand plan for the cultivation of mankind, God created Adam and Eve and after life began on the earth, mankind multiplied. Among many peoples, God selected one nation, Israel, descendants of Jacob. Through the history of the Israelites, God wanted to reveal His glory and providence for the cultivation of mankind not only to Israel but also all the people of the world. The people of Israel thus serve as a model for the cultivation of mankind, and the history of Israel, which God Himself governs, is a history of not only one nation but His message for all people. Moreover, before completing the cultivation of mankind that began with Adam, God has willed for the gospel to return to Israel, from which it originated. However, it is exceedingly difficult to conduct a Christian gathering and spread the gospel in Israel. The manifestation of God's power that can shake heaven and earth is required in Israel, and fulfilling this portion of God's providence is the calling designated for Manmin in the last days.

Through Jesus Christ, God has accomplished the providence of salvation of mankind, and allowed anyone who accepts Jesus as his Savior to receive eternal life. God's chosen people of Israel, however, did not acknowledge Jesus as the Messiah. Furthermore, even until the moment His children are lifted up in the air, the people of Israel will not have understood the providence of salvation through Jesus Christ.

In the last days, God wants the people of Israel to repent and accept Jesus as their Savior so that they will reach salvation. That is why God has allowed the gospel of holiness to enter and spread throughout Israel through a noble calling He has given to Manmin. Now that a crucial steppingstone for Middle East missionary work has been established in April 2003, in accordance with the will of God, Manmin will make specific preparations for Israel and accomplish the providence of God.

The third prophecy concerns the construction of the Grand Sanctuary.

Soon after Manmin's founding, as He revealed His providence for the last days, God gave us a calling for the construction of the Grand Sanctuary that will reveal the glory of God to all the people of the world.

In Old Testament times, it was possible to receive salvation by deed. Even if the sin in one's heart was not cast off, so long as the sin was not committed on the outside, anyone could be saved. The Temple of Old Testament times was a temple in which people worshiped God only by deed, as the law prescribed.

During New Testament times, however, Jesus came and fulfilled the law in love, and by our faith in Jesus Christ we have received salvation. The temple God desires in New Testament times will be built not only by deed but also by heart. This temple is to be constructed by God's true children who have cast off sin, in a sanctified heart and their love for Him. That is why God allowed the Temple of Old Testament times to be destroyed and willed for a new temple of true spiritual significance to be built.

Therefore, people who are to construct the Grand Sanctuary must be deemed proper in the sight of God. They must be God's children who have their hearts circumcised, of holy and clean heart, and filled with faith, hope, and love. When God sees the Grand Sanctuary built by His sanctified children, He will be comforted not only by the appearance of the building. Instead, by the Grand Sanctuary, He will recollect the process in which the

Sanctuary will have been built, and remember each of His true children who are the fruit of His tears, sacrifice, and patience.

The Grand Sanctuary bears a profound significance. It will serve as a monument for the cultivation of mankind as well as a symbol of comfort for God after harvesting good crops. It is built in the last days because it is a monumental building project that will reveal God's glory to all the people of the world. At 600 meters (about 1970 feet) in diameter and seventy meters (230 feet) in height, the Grand Sanctuary is a massive building that will be made with all types of beautiful, rare, and precious materials, and in each piece of structure and decoration, the glory of New Jerusalem, the six-day creation, and the power of God will be embedded. Looking on at the Grand Sanctuary alone will suffice to compel people to feel the majesty and glory of God. Even nonbelievers will be astonished at its sight and acknowledge His glory.

Finally, building of the Grand Sanctuary is the preparing of an ark in which countless souls are to receive salvation. In the last days when sin and evil thrive, as was the case in times of Noah, when people who have been led by God's children He deems proper come to the Grand Sanctuary and come forth to believe in Him, they can receive salvation. All the more people will hear the news of God's glory and power, and they will come and see for themselves. When they come, countless evidences of God will be presented. They will also be taught the secrets of the spiritual realm and enlightened on the will of God who seeks to reap true children resembling His own image.

The Grand Sanctuary will serve as the nucleus of the final phase of the worldwide spread of the gospel prior to the Advent of our Lord. Moreover, God has told Manmin that when the time comes for the construction of the Grand Sanctuary to begin, He would lead the kings and individuals of wealth and power to help with the construction.

From its founding, God has revealed prophecies on the last days and His providence for Manmin Joong-ang Church. Even to this day, He has continued to manifest the ever-increasing power and is fulfilling His Word. Throughout the church history, God has Himself led Manmin in order to accomplish His providence. Moreover, until the moment the Lord returns, He will lead us to accomplish all the tasks He has assigned us and reveal the glory of the Lord all over the world.

In John 14:11, Jesus tells us to *"Believe me when I say that I am in the Father and the Father is in me; or at least believe on the evidence of the miracles themselves."* In

Accomplish
the Grand Sanctuary...

Deuteronomy 18:22, we find, *"If what a prophet proclaims in the name of the LORD does not take place or come true, that is a message the LORD has not spoken. That prophet has spoken presumptuously. Do not be afraid of him."* I hope you will understand God's providence through the power and prophecies manifested and revealed at Manmin Joong-ang Church.

In accomplishing His providence through Manmin Joong-ang Church in the last days, God did not give this church revival and power overnight. He has trained us for more than twenty years. Like climbing a tall and steep mountain and sailing through the tall waves in the rough sea, He has repeatedly led us through trials and, by people who have passed those trials with their firm faith, prepared a vessel that could accomplish the world mission.

This applies to each of you as well. The faith by which one can enter New Jerusalem does not develop or grow overnight; you must always be awake and prepared for the day our Lord will return. Above all, destroy all the walls of sin and, with the unchanging and ardent faith, run toward heaven. When you move forward with this kind of unchanging resolve, God will without doubt bless your soul to get along well and answer the desires of your heart. Moreover, God will give you spiritual ability and authority through which you can be used as His precious vessel for His providence in the last days.

May each of you hold fast to your ardent faith until the Lord returns and meet again in the everlasting heaven and in the City of New Jerusalem, in the name of our Lord Jesus Christ I pray!

:her powerful books from the same author

Heaven I (As Clear and Beautiful as Crystal)
Heaven II (Filled with God's Glory)

A detailed sketch of the gorgeous living environment the heavenly citizens enjoy in the five levels of heavenly kingdoms

---

Hell

An earnest message to all mankind from God, who wishes not even one soul to fall into the depths of hell! You will discover the never-before-revealed account of the cruel reality of Hades and hell

---

The Message of the Cross

A powerful awakening message for all the people who are spiritually asleep; In this book you will find the reason Jesus is the only Savior and the true love of God

---

Tasting Eternal Life Before Death

The testimonial memoirs of Reverend Dr. Jaerock Lee, who was born again and saved from the valley of death and has been leading an exemplary Christian life

---

The Measure of Faith

What kind of a heavenly place is prepared for you and what kind of crown and rewards will you receive in heaven?
This book provides with wisdom and guidance for you to measure your faith and cultivate the best and most mature faith.